Criminology in Focus

Criminology
in Focus

PAST TRENDS AND FUTURE PROSPECTS

A. Keith Bottomley

BOOKS
10 East 53d St., New York 10022
(a division of Harper & Row Publishers, Inc.)

First published in 1979 by Martin Robertson & Co. Ltd., 108 Cowley Road, Oxford OX4 1JF.

Published in the U.S.A. 1979 by
HARPER & ROW PUBLISHERS, INC.
BARNES & NOBLE IMPORT DIVISION
ISBN 0-06-490583-7

Typeset by Pioneer Associates, Croydon
Printed & bound in Great Britain by Richard Clay Ltd.,
at The Chaucer Press, Suffolk.

Contents

To Howard and Duncan

Our role as criminologists is not first and foremost to be perceived as useful problem-solvers, but as problem-raisers.
(Christie, 1971)

Preface

Criminology has been recognised as an academic subject for at least a hundred years, with the systematic study of crime and penal theory going back much further than that under a variety of different labels. Whatever consensus there may have been in the past about this enterprise, and the social implications surrounding it, can no longer be said to exist today. The rapid growth of criminology during the past few decades has been closely associated with an increased perception of crime as a 'social problem', with those countries (such as the United States of America) that have experienced the greatest incidence of crime often being at the forefront of criminological theorizing and research. This association is neither accidental nor particularly surprising. Indeed, the current reappraisal of criminology stems partly from its apparent failure to reduce the incidence of crime in contemporary society. Within the academic world much stimulus has come during the last few years from radical challenges to established patterns of research and theory, with calls for a new critical approach to crime and the organized structure of capitalism (see Taylor, Walton and Young, 1973, 1975).

In this book I shall be presenting a personal assessment of some of the major themes that have engaged the attention of criminologists in the course of the subject's chequered history, and suggesting some possible new directions for the future. Despite a basically critical stance I have tried to be constructive at the same time. More detailed accounts of the substance of criminological theories and the findings of empirical research in criminal justice are available elsewhere, and the reader will be provided with the necessary signposts to complementary sources of background information of this kind. What will be attempted here, in the first instance, is the raising of certain key questions about problems of defining crime as the subject-matter of criminology (Chapter 1) and about the kind of knowledge that can be expected in the search for explanations of crime (Chapter 2). The second half of the book (Chapters 3 and 4) will examine in a rather different way the continuing attempts to study the operation of the processes of law enforcement and criminal justice, suggesting the need to move away from a purely empirical approach towards a more value-focused perspective. Thus my interpretation of the scope of criminology includes not just the conventional search for causes of crime, but also the prior questions of the social and political definitions of crime and the formulation of criminal law, as well as the important issues surrounding the enforcement of law, the administration of justice and the application of penal measures. A central element of the position being advocated is the need for criminology to move beyond its traditional boundaries and method-ology towards a broader definition of the subject as one that properly includes consideration of such matters as the philosophy of social science, the ethics of punishment and socio-political analyses of legal institutions. These aspects can only be hinted at in a preliminary fashion in a work of this scope, but it is hoped that they may provide something of a stimulus for other students of the subject to reappraise their own particular critical and empirical perspectives.

Many of the problems of criminology have stemmed from its claim to possess a monopoly of wisdom; but the study of crime is far too complex and value-laden to be left to any self-defined group of 'expert' criminologists. It is not only academic boundaries that need to be broken down within the subject, but also the equally important obstacles to communication between academics and others, whether practitioners, politicians or ordinary members of the public who after all are the main people involved as victims or offenders — both actual and potential! It still seems to me to be worthwhile to try to encourage a more meaningful dialogue between these various interested groups, in the hope of an increasingly informed public debate in which the sharing of knowledge and the clarification of often conflicting values does not degenerate into personal prejudice and slogan-swapping, but contributes towards a better understanding of the social realities of crime and the appropriate social response to deviance.

Finally, on a more personal note, I must thank the University of Hull for allowing me a period of study leave which enabled me to collect my thoughts together in a rather calmer and uninterrupted fashion than would have been possible in the midst of the many demands of routine work. I am especially grateful to my colleague, Clive Coleman, who cheerfully shouldered a greatly increased burden of teaching and other duties during my absence. My writing inevitably intruded more than it ought to have done upon the time to be shared with my wife and young sons, to whom the dedication will probably seem to be a slight and truly academic recompense in the circumstances.

Cottingham,
East Yorkshire

Keith Bottomley
April 1978

CHAPTER 1

What is Crime?

We must recognise that there are several concepts of crime.
Each concept serves the interests of those who treasure it.
[Quinney and Wildeman, 1977, p. 8]

Crime is a political phenomenon. What gets defined as
criminal or delinquent behaviour is the result of a political
process within which rules are formed which prohibit or
require people to behave in certain ways. [Chambliss, 1976, p.
101]

To pose a question such as 'What is crime?' at the beginning of a
book about criminology might seem to be typical of the way in
which social scientists spend their time asking rather silly questions
to which the answers seem only too obvious. Nevertheless I hope to
show that it is not quite so easy to answer as might appear at first
sight. It is essential to face this question at the outset because
criminology itself can be defined in similar, deceptively simple,
terms as 'the study of crime'. The problems of defining crime and
identifying 'criminals' raise issues that are fundamental to the
present attempt to locate academic criminology within a wider
context.

To begin at the beginning involves an examination of the often
controversial debate during the last hundred years of the development of modern criminology concerning the appropriate focus for
its professional attention; in particular, I shall consider whether
legal or sociological definitions of crime should confine its sphere
of activity. I shall then consider past and present attitudes within
criminology and society at large towards the idea of crime and

1

criminals as essentially 'political' actions and actors. Another recurrent cause for concern in professional and public circles has been the extent of 'undetected crime' in the community, and the significance of this will be examined at both the theoretical and practical levels. Finally, this introductory discussion will be rounded off by an attempt to draw together some personal conclusions about the scope of criminology. Much of what will be said may appear to be too lightly dismissive of the enterprise and achievements of other scholars, past and present. However, at a time when so many societies are conscious of an increasing 'crime problem', it is more than ever important for criminologists to clarify, for themselves and for others who might look to them as 'experts', the nature of their work and the limits of their contribution to issues which properly involve the whole of society.

CONCEPTS OF CRIME IN CRIMINOLOGY

Modern criminology was in a literal sense created in the second half of the nineteenth century on the continent of Europe. In its early days it was dominated by a group of Italian scholars with a 'biological-positivist' or anthropological approach to the subject: Cesare Lombroso (1836-1909), who published the first edition of his influential book *Delinquent Man* in 1876, Enrico Ferri (1856-1929) and Raffaele Garofalo (1852-1934). Many others before them had embarked upon serious and systematic study of crime, including lawyers, philosophers and sociologists, but the distinguishing characteristic of the Italian positivist school was their emphasis upon studying the *individual criminal* and the factors that influenced his behaviour. Their most enthusiastic propagandist, Enrico Ferri, was very anxious to develop a truly professional identity that would clearly mark them out from the earlier classical school of criminal law, represented especially by the writings of Beccaria (1764), whom he accused of 'metaphysical pedantry' in the way they studied crime as infraction and not action and as a 'judicial abstraction', being more concerned with the *diminution of punishment* than the problem of the *diminution of crime* (Ferri, 1913, p. 97). The work of the classical school has been described as 'administrative and legal criminology' (Vold, 1958), and it is clear that their main concern was the reform of the criminal law and the administration of justice; more attention was paid to equating the penalties imposed upon specific criminal acts, as such, rather than to investigating individual motivation. The true measure of crimes in their view was the harm done to society and not the intention of the person who committed them (Beccaria, 1764; 1963 trans. pp. 64-5).

The fact that the term 'criminology' did not gain popular currency until the rise of the positivist school towards the end of the last century with its focus upon the individual criminal is of central significance in understanding the historical development of the subject and the continuing debates within contemporary criminology as to its essential nature and rightful scope. Developed, at least in part, as an entirely self-conscious reaction against the legal orientation of the classical school the Italian school of criminology exhibited an impressive self-confidence in the way it defined the terms of reference for its new descipline. Its anti-legalistic stance was matched only by the obsessive preoccupation with building the framework for a truly 'scientific' enterprise.

Lombroso's original concept of the 'born criminal' (although modified in his later writings) suggested that criminality was due to inherited characteristics of a kind that clearly assumed a certain 'universality' in the anti-social behaviour being explained. Ferri did acknowledge the need to study crime as a legal concept (or 'juridical phenomenon'), but his central message was that 'every case is above all a natural and social phenomenon, and should be studied primarily as such' (Ferri, 1913, p. 57), and that 'the proper subject of criminal anthropology is the anti-social individual in his tendencies and in his activity' (Ferri, 1917, p. 79). The Italian criminologists entertained no doubts about their ability to recognize 'anti-social' behaviour whenever it might appear. There occurs a particularly interesting passage in Ferri's *Criminal Sociology* where he explicitly recognized the very real conflict that can exist between the legal and criminological definitions:

> For the legislator as well as for the judge and public sentiment, a born-criminal may be legally an honest man . . . One may never have violated the penal code and be none-the-less morally and socially a rascal often endowed with brilliant faculties, but certainly worse than many convicts. . . . So delinquency has social equivalents which in the more cultivated classes replace its

brutal, atavic, violent forms with anti-social or immoral forms of activity which circumvent the law without frontal attack. Thus rape becomes seduction: . . . the robber becomes the usurer and the Panama stock-jobber; the yeggman becomes the duelist or the colonial or warlike adventurer.
[Ferri, 1917, p. 79]

Here lies the crux of the criminologist's dilemma: having recognized the 'universality' of certain personality traits and the relatively fortuitous way in which similar behaviour may be interpreted differently according to circumstances and individuals, what criteria should determine whether, why or when particular behaviour should be the focus of study?

Finally, reference must be made to Garofalo's concept of 'natural crime'. Like his colleagues he was dismissive of the purely legal concept of crime, which he saw as being borrowed from popular usage, and he went even further than Lombroso and Ferri in spelling out his special notion of 'natural crime' — 'that which exists in a human society independently of the circumstances and exigencies of a given epoch or the particular views of the lawmaker' (Garofalo, 1914, p. 4). He accepted the impossibility of describing this universal element in crime in terms of specific acts that are regarded as criminal in every society, and instead focused on the *universal sentiments* that he claimed were always harmed by crime:

We must lay aside the analysis of *facts* and undertake that of *sentiments*. Crime, in reality, is always a harmful action, but, at the same time, an action which wounds some one of the sentiments which, by common consent, are called the moral sense of a human aggregation.
[Garofalo, 1914, p. 6]

Garofalo did not claim that a universal morality could be identified, but that there were a number of basic sentiments that could be found across a wide field of human social existence. The details of this concept need not detain us here, but the significance of Garofalo's theory of 'natural crime' lies in the way it epitomized the underlying spirit and ideals of the Italian school of criminologists who were searching for universal laws of human behaviour and had therefore to define their own 'scientific' terms of reference, at the same time as they rejected legal and commonsense usage.

This basic criminological paradigm, established by the early positivists of the biological and anthropological schools in Europe, was not seriously challenged until the publication in America of the report by Michael and Adler, *Crime, Law and Social Science,* in 1933. The main tenets of the critical position adopted by them were that the criminal law was the 'formal cause' of crime, that the only possible definition of crime was the legal one and that criminology should continually strive to live up to its ideals as a developed empirical science. All other possible definitions of crime and criminology were rejected out of hand:

> Attempts have been made to define crime in moral terms and in social terms. The definition of crime as behaviour which is immoral lacks precision and clarity.... The definition of crime as anti-social behavior is hardly more precise or less ambiguous although it does shift the emphasis somewhat from what is thought of as the intrinsic quality of conduct to its social conse-quences.... *The most precise and least ambiguous definition of crime is that which defines it as behavior which is prohibited by the criminal code.*
> [Michael and Adler, 1933, pp. 1-2]

The authors spelled out the logical implications of their position whereby the illegal act itself would be enough to make a person 'criminal', whether or not he had actually been convicted or even whether his crime was known either to himself or to anyone else; but they finally compromised on the safer, pragmatic position that 'unless criminality has been officially determined by the legal processes established for that purpose, it must nearly always remain in doubt' (Michael and Adler, 1933, p. 3). Here we have, at one and the same time, the traditional justification for the reliance in crimi-nology upon the study of *convicted* offenders and also some seeds of doubt about this reliance, hinting at the need to examine the nature and extent of undetected crime and the possible biases within the processes of law enforcement.

It is a nice irony that a central theme permeating the treatise of Michael and Adler was one that they shared not only with the Italian 'founders' of criminology but also with the majority of their later critics. They were absolutely committed to the promotion of criminology as an empirical science, and it was this overwhelming conception that paradoxically influenced their acceptance of the *legal* definition of crime as the only possible operational frame-work:

> Some basis for sharply differentiating criminal behavior from

non-criminal behavior and criminals from non-criminals is a *sine qua non* of the development of the science of criminology. . . . It seems impossible to make this differentiation except in legal terms.
[Michael and Adler, 1933, p. 92, fn. 2]

Precisely the same concern with the scientific nature of criminology was at the heart of Thorsten Sellin's response to Michael and Adler, in his celebrated monograph *Culture Conflict and Crime* (1938). Sellin vigorously reasserted that the scope of criminology should be conceived in strictly non-legal terms; in his opening pages he claimed that 'the term "criminology" should be used to designate only the body of *scientific* knowledge and the deliberate pursuit of such knowledge' (Sellin, 1938, p. 3). Unlike Michael and Adler he had a far from favourable view of criminology as it had developed up to that time, describing it picturesquely as 'a bastard science grown out of public preoccupation with a social plague'. The only way in which criminology could achieve any kind of legitimacy, in Sellin's opinion, was by the application of scientific methods of study to a field of human behaviour to be defined in social rather than legal terms:

> The unqualified acceptance of the legal definitions of the basic units or elements of criminological inquiry violates a fundamental criterion of science. The scientist must have freedom to define his own terms, based on the intrinsic character of his material and designating properties in that material which are assumed to be universal. . . . What *is* claimed is that if a science of human conduct is to develop, the investigator in this field of research must rid himself of the shackles which have been forged by the criminal law.
> [Sellin, 1938, pp. 23-4]

We shall see that thirty years later exactly the same sorts of argument were to be used by those sociologists of deviance who questioned the credentials of criminology as an independent field of study. In 1938 Sellin's less radical objectives were to widen the scope of criminology to focus upon 'conduct norms', which were found wherever there were social groups, and were not the creation or monopoly of any single normative group:

> These facts lead to the inescapable conclusion that the study of conduct norms would afford a sounder basis for the development of scientific categories than a study of crimes as defined in the

criminal law. Such study would involve the isolation and classification of norms into *universal categories,* transcending political
and other boundaries, a necessity imposed by the logic of science.
[Sellin, 1938, p. 30]

There were other American criminologists in the early 1940s who
joined Sellin in advocating wider definitions of their subject matter.
Edwin Sutherland's contribution was especially important in the
way he focused attention on the nature of *social harm.* He raised
questions about the need for a whole new range of activities to
come within the ambit of criminology, leading to the 'discovery' of
white-collar crime in industry and commerce (Sutherland, 1940,
1945, 1949). There was, however, a sharply critical rejoinder to
Sellin and Sutherland by Paul Tappan (1947). Tappan chided those
who wished to stray outside the letter of the law for definitions of
crime, or who wished to study as 'criminals' other persons than
those who had been through the due processes of detection and
conviction. Arguing that broader definitions of 'socially injurious
conduct' were still subject to value judgements, he felt that this
disposed of the argument against the relativity of legal definitions:

Vague, omnibus concepts defining crime are a blight upon either
a legal system or a system of sociology that strives to be objective.
They allow judge, administrator, or — conceivably — sociologist, in an undirected, freely operating discretion, to attribute the
status 'criminal' to any individual or class which he conceives
nefarious.
[Tappan, 1947, p. 99]

Tappan reiterated the point that 'all standards of social normation
are relative' and criminologists should not delude themselves into
thinking that they are replacing the cultural and political value
judgements embodied in the legal code by normative definitions of
social behaviour that are entirely value free.

In the academic climate of the early post-war years, when
criminology was on the threshold of a period of rapid expansion,
particularly in countries like Britain, Tappan's call for a more
legalistic and less sociological orientation tended to be ignored.
Apart from one or two scholars, such as Clarence Ray Jeffery
(1956a, 1956b, 1959a, 1959b), there was little support for a strictly
legalistic approach to the study of crime until the rise of the radical
critiques of traditional criminology in the 1960s. The mainsprings of
these radical attacks were so varied as to preclude any simple

generalizations about a commonly-shared view of the 'legalistic' element in crime and criminology. Paradoxically, one of their main targets was the conservative and institutional basis (and bias) of established criminology — what Matza (1969) called its 'correctionalism' — whereby criminologists, often in the pay of government or social welfare agencies, restricted their study to officially processed offenders. This characteristic feature was seen by some of its most vociferous critics (e.g. Phillipson, 1971) as completely undermining any claim to academic respectability. They ignored the fact that in terms of theoretical objectives criminologists could be accused more fittingly of being too much out of touch with the existing legal framework rather than too much in league with it.

Concern about the effects of the institutional straightjacket of criminology seems to have blinded many critics to the important theoretical issues raised by Sellin and Sutherland, but a significant element in radical criminology is the revived emphasis upon the role of law and legal definitions. In his early writings Jeffery foreshadowed this trend and drew a distinction between theories of criminal *behaviour* and theories of *crime*:

> All of the theories of crime now put forth in criminology are theories of criminal behaviour. Criminologists need a theory of crime, a theory which explains the origin and development of criminal law in terms of the institutional structure of society. [Jeffery, 1959a, p. 534]

He was not just making the superficial 'nominalist' claim that the cause of crime is the criminal law, but he was drawing much needed attention to the fact that a criminology that ignores the origins of criminal law has severe limitations, because 'a theory of behaviour is not a theory of crime'. Jeffery's claim that 'the definition of crime, be it legal or sociological, must be based on a study of law and society rather than on a study of the individual offender' (Jeffery, 1959b, p. 372) summed up the main indictment against the early Italian positivist school of criminology whose over-reaction to the legalistic concerns of the classical school of the late eighteenth century resulted in their concentrating on the behaviour and characteristics of the individual offender to the exclusion of an examination of the origins of the law itself.

Several leading radicals in the United States have followed

Jeffery in the stress laid upon a study of the criminal law, notably Richard Quinney (1964a, 1970) and William Chambliss (1976). Quinney's emphasis upon the fact that crime is a definition of human conduct, if interpreted in a literal and exclusive way to rule out all study of the behaviour of individual criminals *qua* behaviour, would eliminate much of what must still be an integral part of a fully developed criminology, but it is the essential starting point:

> Crime is a *definition* of behavior that is conferred on some persons by others. . . . Persons and behaviors, therefore, become criminal because of the *formulation* and *application* of criminal definitions. Thus, *crime is created.*
> [Quinney, 1970, p. 15]

> Thus to ask 'Why is it that some acts get defined as criminal while others do not?' is the starting point for all systematic study of crime and criminal behavior. Nothing is inherently criminal, it is only the response that makes it so. If we are to explain crime, we must first explain the social forces that cause some acts to be defined as criminal while other acts are not.
> [Chambliss, 1976, p. 102]

A further extension of the radical position on legal and sociological definitions of crime within criminology has come from a recent movement to place at the centre of the subject the issue of *human rights* as advocated in the influential paper by Hermann and Julia Schwendinger (1970), 'Defenders of order or guardians of human rights'. After summarizing the traditional debate on the definitions of crime, they reasserted the importance of moral value-judgements, and went further than earlier formulations of crime in terms such as 'anti-social acts' or 'social injury' by asking how one could determine the meaning of such concepts. In their view the only possible way was by relating the terms to a close analysis of the 'historically determined rights of individuals', so that 'criminologists must be able to identify those forms of individuals' behaviour and social institutions which should be engaged in order to defend human rights' (Schwendinger and Schwendinger, 1970, p. 146). Introducing the concept of human rights would mean that many aspects of social life would for the first time be brought under the umbrella of criminological study, such as imperialism, racism and sexism, while other actions, particularly the so-called 'crimes without victims', would be excluded. Just as there has been a demand for the study of the origins of existing criminal law, so with this new perspective there would be a need to study those institutions and aspects of society responsible for the infringement of specified human rights.

The human rights perspective has attracted considerable support particularly from amongst the ranks of radical and critical criminologists (see Platt, 1975; Quinney and Wildeman, 1977). Others, while basically sympathetic to the humanistic concerns of the Schwendingers, have voiced certain reservations: Hartjen (1972), for example, believed that the proper target of attack was not the legalistic concept of crime itself but the use criminologists have made of it. The Schwendingers combined and thereby confused several elements already present in existing radical critiques — namely, the ideological implications of criminologists' involvement in the fight for 'law and order', and the theoretical aspects of the definitions and goals of criminological study. I would wish to question, as did Hartjen, the purpose served by redefining all infringements of human rights as *crime*. Is it likely they would receive any more public attention or resources for their alleviation as a result of such redefinition? Progress to date in understanding and preventing existing types of crime should not lead us to be very optimistic about the benefits to be gained. It might even detract from the study of these issues in their own right, and could certainly undervalue the essentially political aspect of criminal definitions, to which we now turn, reserving conclusions on this debate until later.

THE POLITICAL ELEMENT IN CRIME

It can be claimed with some justification that *all crime is essentially political* and, at the same time, that *'political crime' is not essentially criminal.* If it is accepted that criminology may, for certain purposes, operate within the established framework of criminal definitions and yet should not restrict its investigations to the individual behaviour of those who come to be labelled as criminals, this means that the nature of the legal definitions and official labels should be subject to careful scrutiny. Such scrutiny can most usefully start with the role of the political element in crime, especially as this continues to give rise to vigorous controversy not only among academic criminologists with their wide range of ideological sympathies but also in national and international politics, law enforcement and the treatment of convicted offenders.

The claim that all crime is essentially political can be viewed simply as a statement that concisely expresses a historical and contemporary fact about the origins and maintenance of legislation, namely that criminal law is the result of a political process whereby organized communities formulate rules and lay down sanctions concerning those actions they wish to prohibit. To describe this process as 'political' may merely be a tautological way of saying that it occurs within the framework of a relatively organized social group.

The truth is, of course, that those who choose to emphasize that crime is political are not usually making an unexceptionable descriptive statement but are keen to draw special attention to the way in which the political process revolves around issues of differential power and consequential bias, in terms of such variables as class, social status, race, religion and sex. Thus historical and sociological analyses of the origins of law are concerned to reveal the particular social groups in positions of power to influence the politics of law-making, and to analyse the extent to which conflict or consensus may be said to exist on the substance of law and law enforcement practices (see Chambliss and Seidman, 1971; Carson, 1974; Chambliss and Mankoff, 1976). Available historical evidence confirms the importance of criminal law in protecting the interests of the social and economic elites (Hall, 1952; Hay *et al.,* 1975; Thompson, 1975), and although the influence of identifiable power groups in society upon contemporary criminal legislation may be somewhat different, the typical *application* of criminal definitions certainly seems to exhibit differential bias (see Box, 1971; Bottomley, 1973).

Attaching the label 'political' to crime in general is a further feature of the critical criminology that has emerged in the last decade, and consequently it is now commonly used with the persuasive purpose of drawing attention to the issues of power, conflict and disadvantage in criminal justice. In Quinney's formulation of a theory of the social reality of crime his first proposition, defining crime as a *definition of behaviour,* was followed by a second according to which 'criminal definitions describe behaviors that conflict with the interests of the segments of society that have the power to shape public policy' (Quinney, 1970, p. 16). This 'interest group' theory of criminal legislation has proved to be particularly adaptable to a Marxist approach to criminology, but it is clearly a theory that must be seriously studied and carefully elaborated in a variety of historical and comparative contexts. Similarly, the work of Chambliss has been invaluable in terms of historical and theoretical analyses of particular pieces of criminal legislation that raise questions of political power and the 'mobilisation of bias' (Chambliss, 1975; 1976).

Among the motives for emphasizing that crime is political is clearly an implicit or explicit demand, at the very minimum, for the recognition of the interests of the not-so-powerful social groups in formulating and applying criminal definitions. The demands often go much further than this, and when associated with the 'human rights' redefinition of crime may call for revolutionary changes in society, indicting the existing legal system not only for being the nominal cause of crime but as essentially criminal itself:

> We need a definition of crime which reflects the reality of a legal system based on power and privilege. . . . The state and legal apparatus, rather than directing our investigations should be a central focus of investigation as a criminogenic institution, involved in corruption, deception and crimes of genocide. . . . Under a radical, human-rights definition, the solution to 'crime' lies in the revolutionary transformation of society and the elimination of economic and political systems of exploitation.
> [Platt, 1975, p. 103]

Another aspect that may help to clarify the ambivalence surrounding the political element in crime relates to the overtly acknowledged and widely used concept of *political crime*. Throughout history, from at least the time of Socrates, there has been an awareness of the existence and social value of so-called 'political criminals'. Even in the relatively short history of modern criminology there has been a recognition of the special class of 'political crimes' that contrasts sharply with the lack of recognition of the broader political basis of 'ordinary' crimes. Among the early pioneers there quickly emerged a polarization in the moral evaluation of the behaviour of 'born criminals', exhibiting pathological anti-social behaviour, and of the completely separate class of 'political criminals' who were often regarded almost as heroes before their time.

Lombroso described political crime as 'a kind of crime of passion, punishable only because it involves an offence against the conservative sentiments of the human race' (Lombroso, 1918, p. 226). He saw it mainly as a crime of the young, especially in those civilized nations where justified changes were necessary in religious and political attitudes and structures; it was a commendable expression of the discontent of large groups in society, often stemming from socio-economic injustices. In line with these sympathetic views on the origins of political crime, he took an unusually progressive line in recommending appropriate sanctions. There should rarely be any question of capital punishment for political criminals or even any severe punishment at all; rather he favoured remedying the economic problems of the country which were the seed-bed, and attempting to channel their altruism into more socially useful directions (Lombroso, 1918, p. 412). Lombroso's recognition of the fact that the protest of political criminals was usually against the specific form of government or social order under which they were living led him to suggest the equivalent of modern deportation to a country to which they could more happily adapt — in contrast to the born criminals, who had shown themselves incapable of adapting to any comparable social environment. Finally, he did not allow the political criminals to escape from the clutches of his individualistic biological theories, but claimed to have found a distinction between the true revolutionaries and the anarchic rebels:

> Those who start great scientific and political revolutions are almost always young, endowed with genius or with a singular altruism, and have a fine physiognomy.... But if from the martyrs of a great social and religious idea we pass to rebels, regicides... and to the anarchists, we see that all, or nearly all, are of a criminal type. These are rebels.
> [Lombroso, 1918, p. 434]

Similar distinctions between the egoistic aggression of the ordinary criminal and the altruistic motives of the political criminal are found in the writings of Ferri. The former, who constitute a majority of criminals, are seen as atavistic types who undermine the conditions of social life for their fellow human beings; the latter, on the other hand, are seen as 'evolutionary, or progressive, abnormals . . . who rebel from altruistic motives against the injustice of the present order' (Ferri, 1913, p. 78). The 'evolutionary abnormals' are seen as instruments of human progress through their intellectual and moral rebellion against existing conditions, and Ferri explicitly recognized the inappropriateness of the label 'criminal' at all in such circumstances for those who could perhaps better be classed with the 'pseudo-criminals'. However, his commitment to the new empiricism compelled him to express doubts about the motivation of certain political criminals:

> Political delicts may be committed and are committed every day, not only by men really misled by political passion (pseudo-criminal), but also by insane, born, occasional, and habitual criminals, who, either by social contagion or through personal circumstances, give their criminal tendencies the form of political crime. In our opinion, therefore, political criminals either are not criminals at all or else belong to one of the five categories of the general classification.   [Ferri, 1917, p. 163]

Here we see an early anticipation of two of the main themes in the discussion of political crime: doubts as to whether or how far the label 'criminal' is appropriate for the genuine political criminal and a sceptical approach to the question of the motivation of those committing apparently political crimes.

Similar views of an entirely contemporary relevance are found in several of the other early criminologists at the turn of the last century. In England, Havelock Ellis saw the political criminal typically as the victimized representative of an oppressed minority trying to overthrow a certain political order that may itself be trying to preserve its own stability by 'criminal' methods — 'the "political criminal" of our time or place may be the hero, martyr, saint, of another land or age' (Ellis, 1901, p. 1). Ellis expressed his views on this subject with a strength of feeling that was as unexpected from him as it was to be expected from the celebrated Dutch criminologist Willem Bonger, who wrote one of the first thoroughgoing analyses of crime from a socio-economic and political perspective. He was probably the first fully to articulate, alongside his views on political crime, a conception of the political nature of crime in general. Bonger believed that crime was not just an 'anti-social act', but that it was specifically harmful or prejudicial to the interests of those groups of persons in the ruling class who exercised the power to define what should be criminal; at the same time, he acknowledged that many crimes were against the interests of all classes in society and would remain so even after a radical change in the political structure (Bonger, 1916, pp. 379-80). Political offenders, in Bonger's opinion, were of a totally different nature from most ordinary criminals; their actions were in no sense egoistic, but they risked their life and liberty for the benefit of the oppressed classes in society, and by extension of the whole of humanity. The political criminal could truly be termed a *homo nobilis,* in contrast to the ordinary criminal — *l'homme canaille* (Bonger, 1916, pp. 648-9)!

It can be seen that, apart from certain residual doubts at the margins of the categorization, the early positivists were uniformly in agreement that 'political crime' had to be treated entirely separately from the rest, both in terms of theoretical understanding and practical policy. In this respect, at least, *they recognized the unambiguously political nature of certain crimes, while simultaneously overemphasizing the basically non-political and anti-social aspects of the majority of crimes.* Not to have recognized such a difference would have required a radical revision of their entire approach to the objectives of criminology, as then defined, with its scientific pretensions:

> From any scientific point of view the use of the word crime, to express a difference of national feeling or of political opinion, is an abuse of language. Such a conception may be necessary to ensure the supremacy of a Government, just as the conception of heresy is necessary to ensure the supremacy of a Church. . . . A criminality which is regulated partly by chronology, partly by longitude, does not easily admit of scientific discussion.
> [Ellis, 1901, p. 2]

Attitudes towards political crime in the 1970s exhibit many of the features found earlier. It is assumed that different sorts of theories are necessary to understand the motivation of so-called political criminals, and in many countries to be officially labelled as such results in special administrative arrangements for purposes of treatment. There are certain sorts of political crime that can be identified relatively easily. These are instances where legislation explicitly proscribes certain acts as directly threatening the political structure or government of the country, such as treason, espionage and the organization of movements of political or religious protest in opposition to those in power. In these circumstances, the proscribed activities are most likely to be committed from overtly political motives, although there are still many problems inherent in the formulation of such legislation and the treatment of such offenders after conviction.

A more problematic category includes those cases where the law invoked is that which covers ordinary crimes, in terms of the alleged harm to human life or property, or breaches of public order. Even Garofalo was aware of this relatively sophisticated (if also potentially disingenuous) justification for treating political offenders no differently from others, and he suggested that a political crime could properly be regarded as a 'natural crime' provided that relevant sentiments of humanity or pity had been wounded (Garofalo, 1914, pp. 37-9). In view of the wide discretion that exists in law enforcement and the criminal justice process it can never be certain how far the law is being applied differentially according to the supposed motives of the accused. Indeed the entire trial process, up to and including the choice of sentence can (and clearly often does) reflect the political element believed to be behind particular actions. Wherever one looks, whether at cases involving Black Power leaders in America or Irish bombers in England, even though the charges may appear as if for 'ordinary' crimes it is impossible to be certain that the political aspects have no bearing on the way the law is enforced. Paradoxically, also, the allegedly progressive movement towards the 'individualization' of justice allows much more scope for political 'bias' than would have been likely under the former classical approach to criminal law, with penalties related to harm done rather than to the needs of the individual offender.

One of the most comprehensive surveys of political crime is by Stephen Schafer (1971; 1974). He was fully aware of the modern trend towards politics becoming more criminalized at the same time as crime is becoming more politicized. He was also firmly convinced of the potential value of political crime in bringing about much needed social change. To mark this particular quality and type of political crime he suggested the term 'convictional' criminal, to reflect the strong convictions they hold of the truth and justifications for their beliefs and actions. In contrast to the egoism of the ordinary offender, usually motivated by purely personal gain, the convictional criminal has an altruism of a non-personal communal kind, in which the interests of specific individuals may be sacrificed in the interests of the long-term social benefits resulting from political change (Schafer, 1974, p. 147). He is convinced of the justice of his cause and believes that only crime can promote it. In this way, the criminal act is not an end in itself but an 'instrumental crime' for ideological goals, often accompanied by a desire to be treated as an ordinary criminal as far as punishment or other public sanctions are concerned.

To anticipate possible objections to this rather idealized image of the genuine convictional criminal, Schafer acknowledged that there may be some who use the political umbrella as an excuse for participating in acts that in their case should be seen as no different from conventional crimes. He felt that such offenders should be called 'pseudo-convictional' criminals (Schafer, 1974, pp. 154-8). Whilst agreeing with Schafer on the importance of devising an objective method of distinguishing the genuine political criminal from the criminal 'hanger-on' if we are to develop an integrated approach to political crime, this task is far from easy in practice. The more doubts that are expressed about the genuineness of the motivation of even just a few political criminals, the easier it becomes for those who wish to undermine the integrity of all political criminals. Once this sceptical position gains any sort of foothold political crime as such can then be explained away, and what Skolnick (1969) has called the 'riff-raff theory' comes into play, whereby an entire political protest movement can be attributed to a minority of troublemakers, who are alleged to indulge in crime for its own sake and are neither genuine in their expressed motivation nor truly representative of any wider constituency.

In this way we begin to see the 'convergence in labels and behaviour' between political protest, social unrest and delinquency, identified by Stan Cohen (1973a). A few years earlier, Horowitz and Liebowitz had drawn attention to the way in which the line between the social deviant and the political marginal was fading, particularly in the context of the black civil rights movement in the United States:

> Originally, there was a clear distinction between vandalism for personal gain and an act of organization for political gain.... The rise of civil disobedience as a mass strategy has blurred this distinction. Such disobedience entails personal deviance to attain political ends. Regardless of the political goals involved, it is conscious violation of the law. The treatment of civil disobedience in the courts has therefore been marked by ambiguity. [Horowitz and Liebowitz, 1968, p. 286]

They went on to claim that 'a well ordered society is one that can impose a distinction between responses to deviance and responses to [political] marginality', although it is not entirely clear whether this call for differential response would ultimately serve the interests either of justice or the political causes being espoused.

Cohen put forward a rather more developed view of the process of convergence between the labels of political and criminal:

> Behaviour which in the past was conceived of as deviant is now assuming well-defined ideological and organizational contours. The politicization of groups such as drug takers and homosexuals is only the most obvious manifestation. . . . On the other side, political marginals such as the Yippies, the Weathermen, the Situationists and the Black Panthers are creating new styles of political activity based on strategies traditionally considered criminal.
> [Cohen, 1973a, p. 119]

Elsewhere Cohen and others have shown how popular interpretations of conventional delinquency, such as vandalism, underplay what can be important 'political' undertones in the motivation and targets for attack (Cohen, 1968; Ward, 1973). There are wide areas of confusion in the way political and criminal images are being reversed, by 'the application to recognised areas of ideological conflict of the language and imagery derived from traditional understandings of deviance, crime and delinquency' (Cohen, 1973a, p. 123); the invocation of the term 'violence' is particularly susceptible to being used to undermine the legitimacy of essentially political acts.

Is there any way of trying to resolve some of the problems surrounding the relationship between political and ordinary crime? We can put on one side that class of political crime which is specified in legislation directed exclusively at activities that are seen as a threat to the security or existence of the state. There is plenty of scope for debate on what should be covered in such legislation and what sanctions are appropriate for those who breach the law, particularly when one is considering political regimes other than one's own! In general, however, the issues at stake here are much more clear-cut and, in theory at least, more open to public scrutiny.

For the rest, a useful starting-point is Schafer's emphasis on the political relativity of all crime. It can be argued that all crimes are political, in so far as they breach a criminal code established to embody and defend a particular value system, based on the interests of those in positions of power and influence. However fundamentally correct such a generic use of the term 'political' may be, it does not help very much to clarify the terms of the current discussion. At the least, we could adopt the suggestion of Schafer so that ordinary offences would be referred to as *relative political crimes* as distinct from the *absolute political crimes,* with clearly expressed political motivations (Schafer, 1974, p. 29). In considering ordinary crimes as 'relatively political' we should always be aware of possible factors in the circumstances giving rise to them, that may be related to the socio-political environment, but should be on our guard against any unilateral imposition of more direct political motivations upon the perpetrators. It is essential to be as honest and as true to the actual phenomena being studied as possible, avoiding the kind of romanticism that Paul Rock has suggested some writers indulge in, whereby all criminals are seen as 'primitive innocents who are engaged in inarticulate political conflict with institutional authority' (Rock, 1973, p. 103). Identification of the absolute political crimes must be based, in the first instance, on the political motivation explicitly expressed by those involved, and by careful search for corroboration of the genuineness of the expressed motivation. It is necessary to avoid prejudging the situation by the application of pejorative labels that either undermine the political status or over-exaggerate the criminal nature of what has been done. Once the political motivation has been accepted (or rejected) as genuine, the final questions to be faced relate to the implications for criminological study and the wider public response.

There has always been an ambiguity and basic unease in society's response to political crime. Except in the most serious cases of treason and espionage, there are bound to be doubts in many minds about the justification for criminal sanctions against those whose essential crime is their 'loyalty' to another cause or political regime. In the group of absolute political crimes where the offence committed is an ordinary crime against persons, property or public order, but where there appears to be genuine political motivation, what difference, if any, should the political element make? As things stand, the authorities seem increasingly inclined to treat political offences officially like ordinary crime. The response of some radicals to this tendency has been, somewhat paradoxically, to call for a redrawing of the boundaries between the way society treats political criminals and the way it responds to conventional criminals — the paradox lies in the fact that it is the same people who are eager to *politicize* ordinary crime, which would have the opposite effect of blurring this very distinction. Indeed, if the authorities were to take a more 'lenient' view of politically motivated offences at the initial stages of deciding whether or not to prosecute, many would not obtain the publicity afforded by criminal proceedings for promoting their cause. Similarly, it may be the case that severe penalties for political offences are as likely as not to have an incentive effect rather than the deterrent effect intended. As far as the official response of the legal authorities are concerned, it seems desirable to deal with such offences in a way that is as comparable as possible with ordinary crimes, at all stages of decision-making. The more movement there is in criminal justice and penal policy of the future towards a system based less on rehabilitative individualization and more on a 'justice-model' approach (see Chapter 4), the greater seems the likelihood of such equalization of treatment occurring. Under such a system, more attention would be paid to the degree and kind of harm occurring than on the motivation of the individual offenders; there would still be problems of standards of comparability, especially in those situations (e.g. aircraft hijacking, multiple-victim bombings) where the harm inflicted or threatened has no exact parallels in the non-political sphere, but the basis for decision-making should be clearer.

Finally, the implications for criminology. If we favour an all-inclusive legalistic framework for purposes of criminological study, then it goes without saying that all crimes come within its purview, whatever the degree of political relativity. The importance of the political element will inevitably shape the nature of criminological investigations into the origins and justification for specific legislation, whether of an overtly political kind or of a kind that only indirectly involves politically motivated offenders. In all countries there is a great need for critical review of existing 'bias' in legislation and administration of justice, considering the extent to which the law either explicitly or implicitly protects the interests of certain classes, races, occupational groups or sex. To the extent that criminology continues to study the individual offender, the prerequisite is an honest awareness of the dangers of wrongly imputing or denying political motivation, or of interpreting social and environmental factors in ways that distort reality.

HIDDEN CRIME: INTERACTION AND SOCIAL PROCESS

The first systematic attempts to measure the extent and nature of crimes committed in the community were made in the first decades of the last century, almost fifty years before the rise of positivist criminology in Italy. This early statistical work is traditionally associated with the names of A.M. Guerry (1802-66) and Adolphe Quetelet (1796-1874), who raised issues about the significance of unrecorded crime that are still of central relevance to criminology today. They recognized that the existence of a 'dark figure' of unknown crimes rendered official statistics incomplete and inadequate as the basis for theories of crime. Once the problems posed by the extent and nature of hidden crime and criminals were recognized, there followed a number of typical responses by the pioneer statisticians of crime in nineteenth-century Europe. The most common response was the working assumption of a constant ratio between the recorded crime statistics and the dark figure of unrecorded crime:

> I do not hesitate to say that all we possess of statistics of crimes and misdemeanours would have no utility if we did not tacitly assume that there is a nearly invariable relationship between offenders known and adjudicated and the total unknown sum of offenses committed.
> [Quetelet, 1831, quoted by Sellin and Wolfgang, 1964, p. 25]

Quetelet, however, admitted that conclusions drawn from official statistics would be 'more or less erroneous', and expressed astonishment that the nature of the relationship between known and unknown crime had received so little attention. In contrast to the healthy theoretical scepticism expressed in his early writings, most of his later practical studies were based on statistics of *prosecuted crimes* as the most appropriate (?) measure of criminality in society, as he claimed to have discovered a constant relationship between the numbers of crimes reported and those prosecuted. He believed this would remain so long as there were no changes in penal policy, the administration of justice or social conditions during the period being analysed (Sellin and Wolfgang, 1964, p. 26; see also van Bemmelen, 1952).

Another more extreme response to the dilemma of the dark figure of hidden crime was to take the legalistic definition of crime to its logical conclusion, so that the only true 'criminal' for statistical and theoretical purposes was the person who had been convicted and sentenced by a criminal court. Sellin and Wolfgang cited the interesting work of the Italian statistician Angelo Messedaglia (1820-1901). On the one hand, his awareness of the issues was remarkably in advance of his time by recognizing the influence of the victim, the agents of law enforcement, the judicial process and the more general attitudes within each community — yet he concluded that the only true definition and measure of crime was the *adjudicated offender*:

> Generally it is true that *no crime can be defined as such until the personal responsibility of the offender has been assessed*. The subjective element is, so to speak, necessarily combined with the objective one and governs it. Therefore, the reality or the absence of the crime can only be determined when a definitive judicial decision is pronounced.
> [Messedaglia quoted by Sellin and Wolfgang, 1964, p. 27 emphasis added]

He drew a distinction between the rates of 'objective criminality' where a crime can be established prior to any prosecution, and 'subjective criminality' which can only apply after judicial proceedings have been completed. Official statistics should, in his view, reflect these two different rates.

A final example of how the early European statisticians attempted to deal with the dark figure is shown by the work of Georg von Mayr. He was conscious of the variations in reporting and prosecuting crime in different communities, but as his research led him to believe, unlike Quetelet, that there was no regular pattern in the prosecution of reported crime, he became the first to rely mainly on statistics of *crimes reported to the police* (see Sellin, 1931). This strategy of getting as close as official records allow to the actual commission of an offence was the one favoured by Sellin himself (Sellin, 1931; 1951), and the official statistics of crimes known to the police were for a long time the basis of most theorizing on crime rates, as were adjudicated offenders (especially those subsequently imprisoned) the main basis for most studies of criminal behaviour.

Within contemporary criminology there is considerable ambivalence towards official statistics, and various alternative measures to tap the pool of undetected crime have been developed. Biderman and Reiss (1967) drew attention to two opposing trends in the study of crime statistics, which they termed the 'realist' and the 'institutionalist' approaches. The realist approach has the longer history, rooted as it is in the work of nineteenth-century statisticians like von Mayr. It is primarily concerned with supplementing police statistics with statistics of unreported crimes, to give a more 'realistic' picture of the amount of criminal behaviour in society. The underlying assumption is that there exists an external, objective 'crime reality' waiting to be discovered, and a belief that the development of 'self-report' and 'victimization' studies has already gone a long way towards uncovering the dark figure of crime and criminality.

The institutionalist approach is of more recent origin, and questions the validity of these realist attempts to reveal previously undiscovered crime in our midst. This approach rejects the idea of statistical approximations to a 'true picture' of the crime problem, and concentrates instead upon the analysis of crime statistics as products of the agencies which handle crime reports and the processing of suspects. Early elaborations of this perspective are to be found in the work of Cicourel and Kitsuse, who summarized their position as follows:

> The questions to be asked are not about the appropriateness of the statistics, but about the definitions incorporated in the categories applied by the personnel of the rate-producing social system to identify, classify, and record behaviour as deviant. . . . *Rates can be viewed as indices of organisational processes rather than as indices of the incidence of certain forms of behaviour.* [Kitsuse and Cicourel, 1963, pp. 135-7]

In his now classic work on *The Social Organisation of Juvenile Justice* (1968, 2nd edn. 1976), Cicourel spelled out the implications of this institutionalist approach for traditional theories of the causes of criminal behaviour, based as they were on crime statistics collected by official agencies and on offenders processed by the official machinery of law enforcement and criminal justice. Before considering whether these two divergent approaches can be reconciled a closer look must be taken at the methods of the realist attempts to improve the reliability of official statistics.

The two most common ways of reaching behind the picture provided by statistics of crimes known to the police are the 'self-report' and 'victimization' studies. A more detailed account of their history and typical findings is given in Hood and Sparks (1970, chs. 1 and 2).

Studies of self-reported crime have featured more and more prominently in-criminological research during the last twenty or thirty years, particularly in the United States but also in Scandinavia and Britain. The majority of studies have collected information on admitted delinquency from juveniles by means of questionnaires or interviews — taking care to preserve strict anonymity. Although there is still a lively debate on certain of the conclusions to be drawn from these studies, especially with regard to the social class distribution of self-reported delinquency compared with that of official statistics, the surveys are unanimous in documenting the tremendous reservoir of 'crimes' and 'criminals' that never become known to the authorities and therefore never appear in official records. Inevitably, this raises questions as to the value of criminological theories and crime control measures based only on the tip of the iceberg, where what is below the surface is not only greater but may in this instance be qualitatively different from that which is in full view. Without imagining that it will in any way provide a complete answer to these basically sound criticisms of the inadequacy of theories and policy that are focused only on officially known crime, it is important to pursue a little further the question of how far crime and delinquency can be said to exist 'objectively' and how far, on the other hand, crime is the result of a complex process of interaction involving 'offenders', 'victims' and law enforcement agencies.

At the simplest level, it is clear that many of the items of behaviour about which respondents are asked in some of these surveys are so trivial or so rarely the concern of the police that their inclusion seriously exaggerates the amount of undiscovered 'crime' in the sample population. Occasionally the researchers themselves have been aware of this, and the better studies have devised a variety of weighted indices, so as not to place sole reliance upon the answers to just a few of the more trivial items.

In *Delinquent Behavior in an American City*, Martin Gold analysed the data to see which items on his checklist might turn out 'not to be offences at all', and concluded that 'half of the acts of property destruction to which our sample initially admitted could not conceivably be called chargeable offences, nor could 25 per cent of the confidence games, nor 20 per cent of the personal assaults' (Gold, 1970, p. 13). In the subsequent analysis one of the indices of delinquency used by Gold (Index F) excluded all those 'offences' which the coders judged were most unlikely to be chargeable by the police and included only those that would clearly have warranted police action if they had been detected. The result was that 28 per cent of the 'offences' admitted by the youngsters could not reasonably be considered 'delinquent acts' (Gold, 1970, p. 25).

The kind of items commonly included in such surveys, but which would probably be discounted using Gold's criterion, are trespass, non-payment of fares, lying, school fights, keeping things that have been found, petty acts of damage, truancy and misbehaviour of various kinds at home. Thus, in the course of the Cambridge Study in Delinquent Development, it was found that nine out of every ten boys in the sample admitted to the more trivial acts such as letting off fireworks in the street, going to X-certificate films under age, travelling without a ticket on public transport and riding a bicycle without lights, whereas less than one in every ten boys admitted breaking into houses or stores (West and Farrington, 1973, p. 154). The more closely such self-report studies are examined, the more doubts emerge about the validity of their claims to be measuring 'crime' — either from a sociological or legal point of view — in any way comparable with official statistics of 'crimes known to the police' or 'persons proceeded against'.

Several criminologists have drawn attention to the need to interpret statistics as representing *behaviour that is responded to,* which can therefore only be properly understood by looking at the interaction between all the parties concerned (e.g. Wilkins, 1965; Wheeler, 1967). In the context of self-report studies Leroy C. Gould (1968) suggested the need for a clear distinction to be made between (1) delinquent acts (i.e. '*all* behavior which is in violation of the law, or other social norms'), (2) official delinquency (i.e. 'behavior which someone has *perceived* as being a violation and has *responded to* as if it were a violation'), and (3) self-perceived delinquency:

> Rather than continue the quest for an adequate measure of deviant acts (i.e. all acts which are in violation of social norms), modify the definition of deviance to include only those acts which are perceived by someone in society and acted upon as if they were deviant. In the case of delinquency, this concept would be defined as those acts which are against the law, committed by

juveniles and acted on by society's agents of delinquency control.
[Gould, 1968, p. 333]

Such an approach, if it were to be taken literally, would render
traditional self-report studies of no value at all for measuring in any
precise way the dark figure of hidden delinquency, as this could
only be defined retrospectively in the light of the known social
response. As it is, even in self-report studies, there is evidence that
in many cases of admitted delinquency the 'offence' was known to a
member of the public or the police, but no further action was taken
towards formal reporting or prosecution. In the Cambridge Study,
apart from the 20 per cent of boys with an official juvenile court
record, a further 14 per cent had experienced 'police contact'
without formal prosecution (West and Farrington, 1973, p. 166);
and in another English study of 1,400 London schoolboys, 13 per
cent had been caught by the police at least once (of whom only half
were subsequently sent to court), but nearly three times that number
(37 per cent) had been caught by someone other than the police —
and presumably not reported to the police at all (Belson, 1975,
pp. 118-22). A study in America, based on self-report data from 847
boys and girls (aged 13-16) was able to relate police detection with
court referral. In this sample of teenagers of whom 88 per cent
confessed to committing at least one *chargeable offence* in the
three years prior to the interview, only 9 per cent reported any
detection by the police during the same period, involving less than 3
per cent of the total number admitted; furthermore, only 4 per cent
were referred to court or appeared in official delinquency records
(Williams and Gold, 1972).

These few examples confirm the evidence from numerous other
studies of police discretion in the handling of suspected offenders
that, particularly in the case of juveniles, official and unofficial
decisions are taken that often result in known offenders being let off
with a warning or official caution, thereby delaying the time when
they may become 'official delinquents' (see Bottomley, 1973, ch. 2).

So-called 'victimization' studies are of more recent origin than
self-report studies (see Hindelang, 1976, chs. 2-3; Skogan, 1976),
and their focus of attention is upon the extent of *unreported crime*
rather than *undiscovered criminals*. By definition they can only
encompass those crimes that can be said to have a specific and
personal 'victim', and in practice usually concentrate on the more
serious crimes. Consequently they omit a wide range of public

order and 'consensual' crimes, and many groups of offence in the discovery of which the police traditionally take the initiative. For these reasons their typical findings are perhaps even more surprising than those of self-report studies. National surveys in America have found that less than two out of every three serious crimes are reported to the police; in certain kinds of offence, such as rape, more remain unreported than are reported to the police, and even in crimes such as robbery and burglary large numbers are never reported by the victims. The two most common reasons for not reporting the crime are a belief that the police will not be able to do anything effective in the circumstances (or will not want to be bothered), and the fact that it is regarded as a private matter for which they do not want to involve the offender in police proceedings. Similarly, Hindelang's recent study of victimization in eight large cities in America revealed that less than half of all personal and household victimizations were reported to the police; the main reasons given for non-reporting were that 'nothing could be done' or the victim did not consider it important enough (Hindelang, 1976, ch. 14; for a unique English study see Sparks *et al.* 1977).

In their review of the evidence from victim surveys in the United States, Hood and Sparks showed that in several instances care was taken to ensure that only 'real crimes' were recorded for comparison with official police statistics. Assessments were made of the legal status of the 'crimes' concerned, the credibility of the respondent and the likelihood of police action, with the result that in one study the research assessors agreed that about one-quarter of all victims' reports were not crimes and excluded them from further comparative analyses; then when lawyers and police officers made further checks on these assessments, they excluded a further one-third of the crimes 'passed' by the research assistant (Hood and Sparks, 1970, pp. 30-1)! It seems abundantly clear that the findings of victimization studies are not to be taken at their face value as estimates of the dark figure of unreported crime. Not only must we examine closely the reasons for crimes not being reported, but we must also consider the evidence of disparities in the definitions and perceptions of victims, researchers, lawyers and police officers.

The criticisms that can be levelled at research attempts (within the 'realist' tradition) to reveal the 'dark figure' of undiscovered crime, by means of self-report and victimization studies, seem to lend more credence to the alternative 'institutionalist' approach whereby, as one writer has put it, 'crime statistics are not evaluated as inaccurate or unreliable' but are treated as 'an aspect of social organization and cannot, sociologically, be wrong' (Black, 1970, p. 734). Empirical investigations into the 'institutional' response to and the organizational processing of crime and suspected criminals are beginning to build up a picture of the complex circumstances surrounding the production of official crime rates.

In the first place, it has been established that as far as concerns those crimes which are recorded as 'known to the police' the role of members of the public (usually as direct victims) in reporting the crime to the police is crucial. Studies in America and Britain have shown that less than one in seven of such crimes are discovered by the police, with the rest being reported by members of the public (Sellin and Wolfgang, 1964; Black, 1970; Bottomley and Coleman, 1976). Thus the police at this stage assume a reactive role rather than taking the initiative in a 'proactive' sense to discover possible crime. It must be stressed, however, that the roles of the police and the public are reversed in certain offences where there may be no specific victim or where the law is enforced almost entirely on the initiative and at the discretion of the police — ranging from motoring offences and breaches of public order, to prostitution, drug-taking and pornography. Once a crime complaint has been received by the police it is usually subject to preliminary investigation before being officially recorded as a 'crime known to the police'. The extent to which police 'write off' crime complaints as 'no crime' or 'unfound' varies according to local policy and practices, but a conservative estimate would suggest that at least 5-10 per cent of reported crimes are subsequently written off the official record (Coleman and Bottomley, 1976; see also Center and Smith, 1973; Seidman and Couzens, 1974). The influence of the wishes of the 'victim' upon police action can often be a decisive factor in the early recording of 'crime' as it is in later stages of the judicial process. There are also, of course, many other situations in which the police are involved in responding to some kind of complaint from members of the public but which they handle informally without even recording a prima facie case of a reported crime to be investigated. In Donald Black's survey of police-citizen encounters in Boston, Chicago and Washington, it was found that in more than 500 incidents observed, in which the police attended in the presence of a complainant, less than two-thirds resulted in the officer writing out an official crime report

(Black, 1970, p. 735). The decisions in these cases were affected not only by the seriousness of the alleged crime but also the relationship between complainant and suspect, and the interaction between the police and the complainant.

The later stages of the processing of suspected offenders have been subject to much more criminological investigation than the very earliest stages of reporting and recording suspected offences. These subsequent stages include police decisions to arrest, the choice of formal or informal dispositions, the charging process and plea negotiations, findings of guilt and choice of sentence. The wide discretion that exists at each of the stages of decision-making allows plenty of room for individual and institutional prejudices to enter so that the final 'products' (in terms of adjudicated offenders) are most unlikely to be representative of the much larger group of persons responsible for the original crimes alleged by members of the public.

It is very tempting, when faced with the dilemma of choosing between the 'objective' realist and the 'subjective' institutional definition of crime and criminals, to opt for the latter. Such a position is supported in their different ways by statisticians of crime like Messedaglia and twentieth-century 'legalistic' criminologists such as Tappan, but it is also compatible with the interactionist or 'labelling' perspective adopted by contemporary sociologists of deviance. The essence of this perspective, as far as the definitions of deviance and crime are concerned, is summed up as follows by one of its chief proponents, Howard Becker:

> Deviance is not a quality that lies in behaviour itself, but in the interaction between the person who commits an act and those who respond to it.
> [Becker, 1963, p. 14]

This central tenet reappears, with only slight variations, in the writings of other labelling theorists like Erikson and Kitsuse, and some of their claims can be seen as very apt summaries of the assumptions underlying many empirical studies of discretion in law enforcement and the application of criminal definitions:

> From a sociological standpoint, deviance can be defined as conduct which is generally thought to require the attention of social control agencies — that is, conduct about which 'something should be done'. Deviance is not a property *inherent in* certain forms of behaviour, it is a property *conferred upon* those forms

by the audience which directly or indirectly witness them.
[Erikson, 1964, pp. 10-11]

A sociological theory of deviance must explicitly take into account the variety and range of conceptions held by persons, groups, and agencies within the society concerning any form of behavior. . . . It must focus specifically upon the interactions which not only define behaviors as deviant but also organize and activate the application of sanctions by individuals, groups, or agencies.
[Kitsuse, 1964, p. 101]

Although inconsistencies can be found in the writings of those who espouse the labelling perspective (such as Erikson shows above in defining deviance both as *conduct* and as a *label,* and in Becker's use of the term 'secret deviance'), their basic message is that *deviance can only properly be defined as a social response* to certain behavior, and *a deviant is a person so labelled.*

It is too simple, however, to view the issue as an exclusive choice between two opposed perspectives. The different approaches only need to be seen as in direct conflict with one another if it is assumed that there is only one kind of question that can properly be asked, whether about criminal statistics, definitions of crime or the nature and scope of criminology. Immediately it is recognized that there are a number of different (and equally appropriate) questions that can be asked about the validity of statistics and a number of different but equally legitimate functions that definitions of crime can serve, then the situation becomes clearer.

In the first place, as Leslie Wilkins (1965) and others have said, there ought to be a clear distinction made between *crime* (= events) and *criminals* (= persons) — despite the fact that there is a fundamental truth in the proposition shared by the legalists and labelling theorists that strictly speaking a crime (event) cannot be said to have occurred until a person has been formally adjudicated as legally responsible for it. Until that final stage has been reached it can always be claimed that the 'crime' may have been committed by someone under the age of criminal responsibility, or otherwise not possessing the requisite degree of criminal intent. We may grant the need for the most stringent inquiry into the matter of responsibility and intent before attaching the label of criminal to a particular person, but do we always need to be bound by such considerations before talking about 'crime' in the absence of any person who committed the act? In what context can there be a legitimate way of talking about crime (events), apart from considerations more appropriate for when a suspect has been apprehended and proceeded against? I would suggest that this context must be derived from an appreciation of those interests that the law is intended to protect, and must be 'victim-oriented', in the sense that it takes its definitions of whether illegal harm or loss has been incurred from the victim's own perception and assessment, hopefully unclouded by 'extraneous' factors such as the expectation of police (in)effectiveness, personal convenience or embarassment, or by a quasi-judicial anticipation of who may have committed the act.

In defining crime and interpreting criminal statistics there is a very real shared interest between members of the public and criminologists. Insofar as the public may look to crime statistics (or the media's interpretations of them), they are particularly likely to be concerned with the information provided about the nature and extent of the risk of victimization for different crimes; their definitions of crime tend to be very pragmatic and self-interested, and many would welcome Stanton Wheeler's call for more 'consumer-oriented' statistics in which crime rates are expressed in ways that would have more meaning for the general public, incorporating 'victim-specific' details (Wheeler, 1967, pp. 322-3). The dominance of offender-specific information in official statistics reflects not only their administrative source and functions, but also encourages the correctional approach within traditional criminology and penal policy, which focuses predominantly on crime as related to criminals (persons). Criminology needs to broaden some of its theoretical concerns so that it becomes consumer-oriented, and focuses on descriptions and interpretations of crime (events) from the perspective of individual and social harm, rather than concentrating all its energies upon the organizational processing of offenders. Not all crimes will turn out to have been committed by legally adjudged offenders, but for many people this fact does little to diminish the significance of the original harm. Especially as the vast majority of officially recorded crimes are never cleared-up by the police, a criminology that seeks to be comprehensive and relevant must address itself equally to the raw material of crime as defined, however inadequately, in the law and the minds of victims, as well as to the behaviour of the relatively few criminals who become subject to official attention. In this way not only would there be new possibilities for social action but also the range of theorizing could be usefully widened from the personal to the situational level:

> The fact that an act is considered to be a crime focuses attention
> on the offender as the cause almost to the exclusion of other
> elements in the crime situation — the opportunities, the physical
> environment, the victim or, indeed, the law itself. The excessive
> emphasis in the past upon the offender has not paid off and if we
> are to deal realistically with crime it is necessary to study less
> romantic and dramatic elements — to emphasize *things* and
> *situations* in relation to *decisions*.
> [Wilkins, 1974, p. 57]

SOCIAL HARM AND THE SCOPE OF CRIMINOLOGY

The early criminological thinkers, like those of the classical school,
did not concern themselves too much with an introspective search
for definitions of crime and criminals. They more or less took for
granted the existing framework of criminal legislation, with its legal
definitions of crime, and worked instead for reforms in the
application of penal sanctions. It was not until the development of
positivist criminology, which studied the individual offender above
all else, that there arose a fervent interest in defining its proper
subject-matter, particularly within the Italian school where Enrico
Ferri took the lead in campaigning for the establishment of its
scientific credentials. This same deep concern for establishing
criminology as an independent science characterized most of the
later scholars who rejected the legalistic approach in favour of
broader sociological criteria. The incredible lengths to which this
has been taken can be seen in a treatise on theoretical criminology
written by Bianchi, as recently as 1956. He began from the premise
that 'criminology is an independent science maintaining a free
position' and that 'it is detrimental to the prestige of a science if its
position and subject-matter are not determined and precisely
ascertained' (Bianchi, 1956, pp. 1-2). He proposed the following
definition of crime:

> Crime is a sinful, ethically blameworthy, defiant and erroneous
> act, eventually prohibited by penal law, at any rate deserving to
> be followed by conscious counteraction on the part of society,
> which in its behaviour-aspects is the evidence of a failure of
> reciprocal socio-physical adjustment of society and the individual,

being a 'deficient' mode of expression by which man runs counter
to his own self.
[Bianchi, 1956, p. 111]

He even apologized for the incompleteness of this definition and
admitted that he was 'not deluded by the belief that, not even
approximately, all the incidentals of crime have been considered'
(?!). There are other somewhat more restrained elaborations of
similar views (see, for example, Znaniecki, 1928; Wolfgang, 1963),
but they all share a determination to prove the scientific respectability of criminology that has been at the root of many of the
disagreements and doctrinal factions within the subject in recent
years.

Invariably the attention of the majority of these would-be
scientific criminologists was focused upon the deviant behaviour of
individuals in society, with the primary objective of developing
theoretical generalizations about such behaviour. It was this
restriction of objectives and subject matter that increased the
pressure to create 'universal categories' of behaviour that were not
artificially constrained by limits of the legal codes of particular
times or places:

> The only reason the issue of a definition of crime is raised in
> modern criminology is that the criminologist has to have some
> device by which to place behaviour in that category before it is
> studied as such. However, the criminologist is in a real dilemma
> in this respect, since as soon as he has derived his universal
> category of behaviour he has lost the very thing he started out to
> study, namely crime.
> [Jeffery, 1959b, p. 10]

Criminologists must come to terms with the fact that there can be
no comprehensive and universal definition of individual criminal
behaviour for purposes of theory construction, as virtually the only
common characteristic shared by the subject-matter of criminology
is that of its being behaviour prohibited by current criminal
legislation. Crime is defined by the criminal law and there are no *a
priori* reasons why, beyond that definitional element, either crime
or criminals should possess anything more substantial in common.

The starting-point for criminology, therefore, must be the study.
of the historical and socio-political processes which have given rise
to criminal legislation at different periods of time and in different
societies, recognizing the political relativism of all crime along with

the more absolute political nature of certain offences. Criminology must not rest content with simply studying past and present influences upon the formulation of criminal law, but it must also contain an internal dynamism for the constant evaluation of the scope of the criminal law and for working towards penal change in a deliberately self-conscious fashion.

In my view, an adequate grasp of the scope of academic criminology can usefully be based upon a reconsideration of some of the key elements involved in the emergence of the socio-legal concept of crime. Historically, before the state as such became directly involved in crime control, most of the injuries to life and property that are now criminal were sorted out on a personal or family basis (Jeudwine, 1917, pp. 64-5). The interests of the victim and his kinsfolk were paramount to such a degree that Stephen Schafer referred to this early communal period as 'the golden age of the victim' (Schafer, 1968, p. 14). Virtually all social delicts were treated as torts, with the actual harmful consequences of the act being all important for the awarding of compensation, but other elements of punishment and concern for the intentions of the actor were disregarded.

In the Western world the change from the concept of tort to that of crime took place in the early Middle Ages, when for a variety of religious, political and social reasons most such acts became redefined as crimes, with which it was the state's business to deal. From this time onwards the concept of crime became increasingly complex, with important religious overtones as well as sometimes rather dubious claims as to the state's role as the chief victim. Many of the penalties remained the same, such as death, outlawry and payment of money, but this was now paid as a 'penalty' to the state not as restitution to the personal victim; the initiative in taking action against offenders passed from the kindred of the injured party to the king or state's representative as public prosecutor (Jeudwine, 1917, p. 85). The decline of the role of the victim in criminal justice had set in and was to last for many centuries until some signs of a possible revival in the present day (see Chapter 4).

The assumption of responsibility by the state for criminal jurisdiction immediately introduced the political relativism of crime. No longer need there be sole reliance upon the personal victim's awareness of harm suffered and a desire to seek recompense, but the definition of harm was taken over by the law-maker and the law-enforcers, in such a way that it could be extended and used to protect the interests of those with influence in the state. The consciousness of the political element in crime that was very strong in the Middle Ages can be associated with what Schafer called a 'suprauniversalistic' concept of crime, whereby the notion of a victimized ideology replaces the concept of the personal victim and gives rise to the idea of a more metaphysical victim of the state and the community (Schafer, 1968, p. 36). Unfortunately the idea of 'social harm' or damage to the community can and has led to considerable confusion and mystification about the purposes of criminal law and the interests not only of the victim but of the other diverse groups in society (see Eser, 1966). Paul Rock considered the relationship between law and authority and concluded:

> It may well be true that most criminal laws are, in fact, instrumental in preventing social harm. Yet it is mistaken to assume that law is enacted solely from a position of Olympian detachment. The transformation of behaviour into *crime* must be understood largely as a result of a moral world's active inter- pretation of that behaviour. It cannot be usefully discussed as if it were no more than a straightforward and rational response of a society to threatening acts. The emergence of law is founded on processes which mediate between behaviour, its construction as threatening by the powerful, and its translation into crime. [Rock, 1973, p. 149]

Whether we look at socially injurious acts from the point of view of the victim (if any), the intentions of the actor, or in the light of the nature of the harm done, it seems clear that there is no hard and fast distinction between torts, crimes and non-criminal harm (see Hall, 1960; Mueller, 1955). In practice there is a very blurred demarcation line between those acts or omissions which are the concern of the civil law and of the criminal law — or no law at all. The main difference lies not in the act but in the consequences to the perpetrator: the civil law regarding torts is concerned exclusively with compensation to the person who suffered the damage, whereas criminal law is traditionally concerned above all with punishment and prevention of future crime, and only marginally with restitution to the victims of crime (see Chapter 4).

Mark Kennedy examined the extent to which independent features of crime could be identified. As we have seen, 'harm' is not an exclusive characteristic of crime, nor is personal victimization. Not all crimes need to be shown to be committed with deliberate intent provided that certain harm has occurred:

The only criteria which determine whether any behaviour is civil or criminal are not behavioral criteria . . . but are external criteria applied by the State — chiefly, politicality and penal sanction . . . In short, crime has nothing to do with the fact that one person may intentionally harm another but everything to do with the manipulation of law, with the application of criteria *external* to the acts of harm themselves.
[Kennedy, 1970, pp. 53-8]

It is not surprising that this confused state of affairs has resulted in criminology's need to define its own terms of reference. There will continue to be vigorous debate about the 'decriminalization' of certain crimes, especially those bordering upon central issues of personal morality, ethics and religion. There will also continue to be a debate about the inclusion within criminology (and the scope of *criminal* law) of harms that are seen to be particularly damaging to society and requiring punitive or preventive sanctions, or demanding some form of 'denunciation' (see Eser, 1966). The long-running conflict surrounding the concept of white-collar crime is just a single instance of the kind of discussion that is necessary if criminology is to remain responsive to changes in society and social mores.

In terms of objective 'social harm' there can be little doubt that much 'white-collar crime' merits the criminal label, just as do many of the social phenomena referred to by Schwendinger and Schwendinger (1970), e.g. pollution, political aggression, racial and sexual inequalities; similarly, there are precedents in 'absolute liability' offences not to require all crimes to be deliberately intentional harms. The fact that many of these activities have no clearly identifiable 'victim', who is able or likely to take action, can be an argument in favour of the criminalization of the activity in the hope that the state will then take the initiative in enforcement. Sutherland said about white-collar crime that 'it is not ordinarily called crime, and calling it by this name does not make it worse, just as refraining from calling it one does not make it better than it otherwise would be' (Sutherland, 1940, p. 5); similarly, in his critique of the Schwendingers, Hartjen concluded:

I have no doubts that the study of racism and the like is humanistic. I do however question the necessity and the desirability of defining crime in terms of the conditions the Schwendingers suggest. Racism, sexism, imperialism and the like are phenomena that are

objectionable in their own right. It is not necessary to define them as crime (or anything else for that matter) because they are phenomena that, as such, deserve the attention of sociology (and criminology).
[Hartjen, 1972, p. 66]

Some of the most sensible comments to appear in the white-collar crime debate that have a wider relevance are in the paper, 'White-collar crime and social structure', by Aubert (1952). He argued that for purposes of theoretical analysis it was important to utilize concepts that preserved and emphasized the essentially ambiguous nature of white-collar crime, rather than trying to solve the problem by unilaterally classifying them as 'crimes' or 'not crimes'. A study of what Quinney (1964b) preferred to call 'occupational deviance' provides a crucial opportunity to study this essential ambiguity among the public and the businessmen, and among lawyers, judges and criminologists (Aubert, 1952, p. 267). He put his finger on a crucial aspect of the debate among criminologists about what they should study:

> The definition of an activity as 'crime' is always, apart from its scientific merit, a 'persuasive definition'. It contains an element of propaganda. The terminology one accepts in the present controversy will depend upon how much one wants to get rid of these white-collar activities.
> [Aubert, 1952, p. 266]

This goes to the heart of the matter. What criminologists want to define as crime is affected not only by 'objective' considerations of the demands of their discipline as they see it, but perhaps to a greater extent by their subjective value judgements as to the moral or social harm of certain activities, and a desire to control or suppress them. Personal and social values have a central role in criminology, as in other social sciences, and it is important to acknowledge this openly, instead of striving to maintain a spurious front of scientific objectivity. The debate as to what should or should not be regarded as criminal must always be seen as part of criminology, but I see no reason either on moral or pragmatic grounds for being too eager to officially 'criminalize' everything that one disapproves of in society. Many kinds of moral, personal and social evaluations or labels are of more significance than that of the label of 'crime', both as expressions of disapproval and in terms of the possible effects on the individuals concerned. Indeed the popularity of certain crimes, such as motoring offences, is likely to devalue any stigmatizing or preventive effect that the criminal label might have in general. The apparent lack of success of centuries of criminalizing conventional crimes in preventing such behaviour should warn against the easy assumption that once behaviour is made illegal it will immediately disappear.

It may be that for the foreseeable future criminologists will have to accept that the public still holds to a very personalized view of crime and victimization, and are very slow to associate many of the more recent 'social harms' with these traditional categories. There is still something rather paradoxical about the obstinate reluctance of the public to view motoring offences as criminal, despite the very obvious harm they cause directly and indirectly (see Ross, 1960). The diagnosis and the unanswered questions spelled out by Leslie Wilkins sum up the dilemma:

> There seems to be a need to keep crime visible — to personalize it in terms of the criminal. . . . Making roads safer does not have the symbolic appeal of bringing a villain to justice . . . the one villain can be identified, the collective villains can hide. There is little chance but that the public will continue to be persuaded more by symbols of harm which they can see, than by discussions of harms which are invisible. . . . How can we develop and put into effect a rational view of collective responsibility and collective guilt? [Wilkins, 1973, pp. 24-5]

Of one thing at least I am sure, the task is not only or mainly for criminology; there is already too much shelving of responsibility by society for ordinary crime and a blinkered faith that the problem can be solved primarily by action against detected criminals. Formulating the issue of crime control in terms of sanctions against individual offenders distorts and oversimplifies the situation and almost certainly delays the discovery of effective measures for reducing crime.

CHAPTER 2

The Search for Causes

The mere existence of something called criminology perpetuates the illusion that one can have a general theory about crime causation. [Cohen, 1973b, p. 622]

Theories, on the other hand, may serve to exculpate a particular social system, to excuse it from responsibility for those gaps between the 'real' and the 'ideal' that exist within it. [Connor, 1972, p.16]

The chief legacies from the 'founding fathers' of positivist criminology were an emphasis upon the study of the individual offender and a persistent but vain search for a single theory of criminal behaviour. Nigel Walker compared the situation to mediaeval alchemy by referring to it as the search for the 'criminologist's stone'; and in a similarly picturesque way he referred to single-factor theories as the 'monoliths' of a criminological 'Stonehenge Era' (Walker, 1966; 1974).

The best known 'monolith' is probably Lombroso's theory of the 'born criminal', even though he was not the first to put forward such a biological interpretation of crime and quickly modified his own ideas, so that he subsequently regarded only a minority of criminals as being of this type. Monolithic theories of crime in the early part of the present century continued to be predominantly of a biological or constitutional kind, including factors such as mental and physical deficiency, low intelligence and the direct inheritance of criminal traits. Although these approaches to the study of crime still have their modern counterparts in research into somatotypes, chromosome abnormalities, maternal deprivation, conditioned learning

39

etc., such factors are now rarely put forward as single all-embracing theories of crime.

More commonly, during the last fifty years, the 'criminologist's stone' has assumed a sociological shape, with general theories such as Sutherland's 'differential association' and Merton's 'anomie' theory having pride of place. These reflected the beginnings of a move away from single-factor to single-theory approaches, which has culminated in a variety of perspectives adopted by modern radical criminology, such as 'labelling', interactionism, phenomenology and social conflict theories of deviance. Apart from these recent trends, the other more traditional responses to the collapse of the early criminological monoliths have included the rise of multi-factor approaches and the increased popularity of typologies, in which crime is subdivided into several different categories each with its own explanation.

Throughout most of the search for causes of crime by criminologists, a concern with establishing the scientific status of their subject has never been far below the surface. We have already seen how this influenced the debate about the sociological and legalistic definitions of crime, and it has exerted a similarly pervasive influence upon the attempts to discover the causes of crime. Paradoxically, in view of the ideals of 'scientific objectivity', a major preoccupation has been to provide theories which would at the same time be of direct relevance for the prevention, control or treatment of crime. We have thus witnessed the parallel development of a positivist criminology obsessed with the respectability of its scientific credentials and yet, that same criminology proclaiming objectives of a 'correctional' nature for the control of crime in society.

Another key aspect of any attempt to understand theoretical developments within criminology is the recognition that, just as it has often been claimed that 'societies have the criminals they deserve', so also can the equally significant claim be made that *societies have the theories of crime they need.* The social origins and context of different approaches to theorizing about crime and criminals must be considered as a necessary preliminary to more substantial examination of the objectives, assumptions and methods of those theories.

Arguably the most important question to be faced relates to the inherent ambiguity of the concepts of 'cause' and 'explanation' in the social sciences, particularly in comparison with the physical sciences towards which criminology has so often looked for appropriate models. If criminology is regarded as firmly located within social science much of its past failure to discover any acceptable general theory of crime is understandable, particularly given the legalistic and politically relative nature of its subject-matter. After first sketching something of the social context and limited achievements of past theorizing in criminology, we shall consider the nature of explanation in more detail.

THE SOCIAL CONTEXT OF CRIMINOLOGICAL THEORIES

I do not intend to provide a lengthy catalogue of the various theories that have been suggested during the last two hundred years for explaining crime in all its manifestations. Comprehensive historical surveys already exist (see, for example, Vold, 1958; Mannheim, 1960, 1965; Radzinowicz, 1966; Schafer, 1969). What does need more emphasis than it has usually received is the symbiotic relationship between the origins and popularity of particular theories and the wider climate of opinion in society about deviance and the social response. Viewing theories in this way by no means explains them away or eliminates the need for assessing them against other criteria, but it enhances our understanding and should dispel any expectations of 'natural progression' in the way theory supercedes theory.

Social attitudes towards crime in the nineteenth century lend themselves particularly well to this kind of analysis. Several important elements were identified by Leon Radzinowicz (1966), and although he placed more stress on the purely academic 'climate of opinion' at the time, he also considered a broader spectrum of attitudes towards the so-called 'dangerous classes' at the beginning of the century. A fascinating analysis of the intertwining strands of contemporary popular, literary and academic attitudes to crime was provided in the study by Louis Chevalier. The popular conception of the source of the crime problem in early nineteenth-century Europe was overwhelmingly one of an identifiable 'criminal class' or 'dangerous class'. Chevalier showed how in France this older stereotype of crime and criminals predated the first systematic statistical studies of crime by Guerry, Quetelet and many others, but was reflected and elaborated in the early writings of social novelists like Balzac and Janin (Chevalier, 1973, p. 67). According to this view, entry into the dangerous classes was accounted for 'naturally' by a process of economic and demographic determinism, and their rejection by society was symbolized by their physical location in specified parts of all the major cities. Their situation was rarely explained in terms of social changes taking place in contemporary urban society, but was seen in terms of moral pathology and differentiation from the rest of society:

> The dangerous classes are still apart from the other classes, forming a separate people wholly isolated by its customs, speech, history, mode of life and death, and the places where it ordinarily lives out and ends its existence.
> [Chevalier, 1973, p. 73]

> It served the interests and relieved the conscience of those at the top to look upon the dangerous classes as an independent category, detached from the prevailing conditions. They were portrayed as a race apart, morally depraved and vicious, living by violating the fundamental law of orderly society, which was that a man should maintain himself by honest, steady work.
> [Radzinowicz, 1966, p. 38]

A gradual transformation occurred in the second quarter of the century, as surveys of crime and social conditions appeared, rendering no longer tenable the view of neat distinctions between the 'dangerous' and 'labouring classes', or between crime and poverty or social disadvantage. The social surveys of Villermé, Frégier and Buret in France confirmed the close link between the 'criminal classes' and the general urban working classes. This 'progressive transformation of the criminal theme into the social theme' was more rapidly reflected in the contemporary literature of Balzac and, above all, Victor Hugo's *Les Miserables,* than it was recognized by politicians and social reformers (Chevalier, 1973, ch. 5).

This was the context of the statistical studies of crime carried out by Quetelet and Guerry in the 1830s and 1840s, who for the first time systematically analysed the trends and patterns of recorded crime and whose work can lay better claim for the title of 'fathers of criminology' to be assigned to them than to the Italian positivists of the next generation! They concluded that crime was the result of

social causes, and Radzinowicz summarized their contributions as
follows:

> For the first time in the history of human thought crime came to
> be viewed as a social fact primarily moulded by that very social
> environment of which it is an integral part. Never before had such
> persuasive evidence been forthcoming that 'society carries within
> itself, in some sense, the seeds of all the crimes which are going to
> be committed, together with facilities necessary for their develop-
> ment' (Quetelet, *Physique Sociale,* 1869, p. 97).
> [Radzinowicz, 1966, p. 35]

The implications of their findings for a radical reassessment of
society's responsibility for its own crime were enormous and clearly
much less palatable than the idea of a 'dangerous class' which had
only to be identified and then kept at a distance. The social and
political unpalatability of these early criminological surveys almost
certainly encouraged the development of the themes of the moral
depravity and biological 'atavism' of the criminal classes (and the
poor) which dominated the second half of the nineteenth century.

In view of the extensive statistical and sociological studies of
crime that had been carried out in England and France by the
middle of the century (see Morris, 1957) and which looked set to
establish a respectable sociologically-based criminology, is it enough
to account for their sudden demise by showing how Lombroso's
theory of biological atavism mirrored fundamental folk images of
crime and let society off the hook as far as social reform for the
reduction of crime was concerned? Although from a position of
academic detachment it is tempting to agree with the view that 'in
the evolution of criminological theory, it would appear that the
work of Lombroso was in the nature of an interlude and interruption'
(Lindesmith and Levin, 1937a, p. 815), yet the rise and influence of
the Italian positivist school cannot be dismissed quite so simply. A
paper by Lindesmith and Levin on 'The Lombrosian myth in
criminology' suggested a plausible explanation. The authors accepted in part the conventional arguments for recognizing the intellectual background of Lombroso, in the growing popularity of
Darwinism, phrenology and anthropology, but the new elements
they introduced into the argument revolved around the professional
and institutional interests served by this approach to the study of
crime:

The growth of the Lombrosian myth is to be accounted for,

basically, not so much in terms of the acceptance or rejection of theories or methods of research as in terms of a changing personnel. . . . The Lombrosian myth arose, therefore, as a result of the 'seizure of power' so to speak by the medical profession. Medical men compiled bibliographies and traced the history of criminology as a branch of medicine through the works of Gall, Lavater, Pinel, Morel, Esquirol, Maudsley etc., ignoring the voluminous sociological literature.
[Lindesmith and Levin, 1937b, p. 669]

Lindesmith and Levin claimed that the myth that Lombroso was the founder of criminology was mainly a product of America, where the biological-positivist views of crime were allowed to spread virtually unchallenged, in the absence of the kind of theoretical sociological knowledge and research tradition that had developed in Europe. Once the Italian positivist approach had been initially adopted it very rapidly became the institutional foundation of criminology throughout the United States. The American Institute of Criminal Law and Criminology was founded in 1909, under the auspices of Chicago's Northwestern University, which also established the *Journal of Criminal Law and Criminology*. One of the first tasks undertaken by the American Institute was the translation into English of selected European criminology texts for their Modern Criminal Science series. This included the major works of Lombroso, Ferri and Garofalo but completely ignored the earlier statistical work of Guerry and Quetelet — most of which remains untranslated to this day.

The Italian positivists cannot, of course, escape some measure of responsibility for their attitude towards their predecessors. It is not just the way in which Ferri especially was concerned to make exclusive claims for the 'positivist revolution' in the study of crime, but his overwhelming interest in juxtaposing the new doctrines not to the statistical and sociological approaches adopted by French and English scholars in the first half of the nineteenth century, but to the classical school of criminal law, that flourished at the end of the eighteenth century and was dominated by Italians such as Beccaria and Carrara. In Ferri's lectures, published as *The Positive School of Criminology* (Ferri, 1913), the main themes were the failure of the doctrines and practices of the classical school to stem the rising tide of crime, and the favourable way in which positivist theories compare (exclusively) with those of the classical school.

With hindsight we can readily accept the importance of the kind of institutional factors suggested by Lindesmith and Levin as crucial to the full appreciation of the growth of the 'Lombrosian myth'; similarly, with the relationships between popular images of crime, statistical surveys and political constraints surrounding the concept of the 'dangerous classes', as illustrated by Chevalier and Radzinowicz. The more complex history of the development of criminological theory and social attitudes towards crime in the present century lends itself less readily to analysis of this sort. However, it seems likely that broadly similar processes are at work, leading to the view expressed by Wheeler that 'far from moving in a steady and unwavering path toward the truth, the knowledge that develops in a given field will be shaped by a variety of social conditions and influences external to the science itself' (Wheeler, 1962, p. 139). It has only really been with the rise of radical criminology that there has been a renewed interest in the critical analysis of the social origins and institutional bases for criminological theorizing, exemplified in Britain by Stan Cohen (1973b, 1974) and by Taylor *et al.,* (1975).

The major influences include inter-professional rivalries, especially between sociologists and psychiatrists, where the typical conflict not only revolves around the predictable 'struggle for influence' but also reflects different professional objectives. Secondly, there is the influence of the broader climate of opinion in society about individual and social responsibility for crime, with direct implications for the way different theories are likely to be encouraged, ignored or accepted as a basis for political action. Each professional group or academic discipline is also affected to some extent by internal developments and intellectual fashions of its own.

After Lombroso's original theory of the 'born criminal' had been finally discredited in the early years of the present century (Goring, 1913), there was something of a hiaitus in criminology, temporarily filled by theories stressing the role of mental deficiency and low intelligence. However, the 1920s and 1930s saw the parallel development in the United States of sociological theories, derived from the school of urban sociology and ecology at Chicago University, and psychiatrically oriented theories developed mainly by those directly involved in the treatment of 'disturbed' or delinquent offenders. Wheeler attributed the lack of attempted integration between these two major branches of criminological investigation not just to the 'divergence of interests, the type of delinquents studied, and differences in the setting within which observations were made', but more importantly to: (1) sociologists' struggle for a distinct identity and secure position in the academic marketplace; (2) psychiatrists' self-confident complacency, which made them disdainful of the contributions of other disciplines; (3) the development of social psychology within sociology, acting as a 'half-way house' that precluded the necessity of more direct links with psychiatry; and (4) the stress upon empirical validation in sociology in preference to the vaguer 'clinical' methods of psychiatry (Wheeler, 1962, pp. 143-5).

Early post-war criminology in the United States was shaped by academic developments within sociology and by its increasingly 'official' role in the struggle for 'law and order'. Major, but not always continuous, strands of sociological theorizing about crime sprung from Sutherland's theory of 'differential association' and Merton's reformulation of Durkheim's 'anomie' theory. Common features of these two theories included the 'normalization' of crime, in the sense that criminal behaviour was no longer seen as a sign or consequence of individual or social pathology (but explicable as a form of normal learned behaviour — given the right social milieu); in addition, the implication of both theories for social action was to allocate the 'blame' for crime fairly and squarely upon the socio-economic and political organization of society.

Sutherland first put forward his theory in 1939, following his biographical study of a professional thief (Sutherland, 1937), and it was expanded in later editions of his textbook on *Principles of Criminology* (1947, onwards). Many of the central tenets of the theory were derived from the 'laws of imitation' put forward by the French criminologist Gabriel Tarde (1912). Differential association theory has experienced a somewhat chequered history: it gained an initial impetus perhaps because it was one of the very few 'general theories' of crime put forward at the time, and by a criminologist with a growing reputation. In the 1950s and early 1960s it suffered set-backs due to the difficulties of operationalizing the key concepts in a suitable way for empirical validation, but there has been a certain revival of interest recently, perhaps partly due to the findings of self-report studies that, statistically speaking, crime is much more 'normal' than traditionally believed, and partly due to renewed interest in those types of professional and organized crime that were at the root of Sutherland's original work.

Just as Sutherland was indebted to Tarde, so to an even greater extent did Merton draw on the work of the French sociologist Emile Durkheim in his reformulation of 'anomie' theory (Merton, 1938). He suggested that there were different patterns of adaptation to social life, ranging from conformity and ritualism, through innovation, to rebellion and retreatism. These patterns were shaped by the fact that American society set up certain ideals of individual success (largely measured in financial terms) but failed to ensure that society was structured so that there were equal opportunities for each member to achieve these ideal goals.

This same theme of *structured inequality of opportunity* was combined with the problems of conflicting social class values and objectives in a series of studies of delinquent gangs in the 1950s, by Cohen (1955), Miller (1958) and Cloward and Ohlin (1960). But more was involved in this growing criminological interest in juvenile gangs than simply a 'logical' extension and combination of earlier ecological studies with Mertonian anomie theory, as Wheeler reminded us:

> The most important stimulus for gang delinquency studies probably lies with changes in the society and especially the mounting degree of concern for serious and violent gang activity — a concern that has grown steadily since World War II. These changes are most directly reflected in the flow of federal funds into delinquency research and large scale preventive efforts. . . . As gang delinquency became a subject of mounting public concern, the field of social work developed new methods of response. . . . These shifts also indicated a shift in orientation on the part of social workers toward a more sociological view of delinquency causation, and thus made it more feasible to gear sociological research into the applied programs of control.
> [Wheeler, 1962, pp. 148-50]

This interpretation by Wheeler portrays clearly the typical links between theory and practice in criminology and crime control.

The development of criminology in Britain in the post-war period has seen little theorizing that has not been highly dependent upon trends in American criminology. Possible exceptions include the theory of 'maternal deprivation' originally put forward in 1944 by John Bowlby, and subject to considerable modification and criticism in succeeding years (see Wootton, 1959; Bowlby, 1965; Rutter, 1972), and the somewhat maverick work of Eysenck on learning theory and crime (Eysenck, 1977). These indigenous theories, which locate the seeds of subsequent delinquency and maladjustment in early childhood experiences of separation and socialization, aptly symbolize the early institutional dominance of the psychiatric approach to the study of crime in Britain. Cohen (1974) described the close involvement of psychiatrically-oriented criminologists in the formation of the Institute for the Scientific Treatment of Delinquency, which in turn founded what is still the only specialized criminology journal in the country, the *British Journal of Criminology* (or *British Journal of Delinquency* as it then was). The fact that these approaches do not have high-standing within contemporary criminological circles attests not only to the academic developments within their parent disciplines of psychiatry and psychology, but also to the way in which British criminology has gradually become more sociologically-oriented, incorporating perspectives from social administration, sociology of deviance and, latterly, sociology of law. In sociological terms, early research by a handful of British criminologists followed in the wake of the ecological studies of urban crime pioneered in Chicago during the 1930s. Starting with the work of Mays (1954), Morris (1957) and Jones (1958), there has been a degree of academic continuity that has culminated in the on-going study at Sheffield University of urban crime (see Baldwin and Bottoms, 1976). This development has been accompanied by a growing concern with the role of social policy in the welfare state, with 'planned criminal areas' and 'problem' housing estates constituting recurrent themes of public and political debate.

A variety of critical and politically radical perspectives upon crime and penal policy in the last ten years has brought together sections of academic criminology on both sides of the Atlantic in a way that has rarely occurred before. A crucial difference between attempts to analyse and account for the origins of the various branches of radical criminology today and in the past lies in the fact that the new criminological views do not to the same extent reflect widespread 'popular' views about the causes of crime, and measures of social intervention (or 'non-intervention' — see Schur, 1973). Indeed the complex social structure of modern societies, as well as internal developments within criminology, make it most unlikely that there will ever be a return to the apparent homogeneity of attitudes that once existed, so that any contemporary analysis of the social context of crime theories must be much more fragmentary and partial.

Finally, it is important to remember that crime and deviance are not the sole prerogative of Western capitalist democracies. For example, available information about theories of crime in the Soviet Union confirms the need to have regard to the socio-cultural and political background. Walter D. Connor has provided invaluable comparative illustrations of the thesis, both with regard to Soviet attribution of criminogenic factors in capitalist societies but, more pertinently, with regard to theories about their own 'residual' deviance:

> The causes of crime and other ills may be externalized, spatially or temporally: the influence and machinations of other societies or the weight of past history may be cited to show that the *present* social order in a particular nation-state bears no responsibility for such problems. . . . By selection of a particular focus, theories may also deflect attention from the macrostructural properties of a society and turn criticism instead toward less general character-istics, labelling these as departures from the ideal blue-print and blaming them for deviance.
> [Connor, 1972, p. 16]

Connor's study showed how the orthodox view was that 'the socialist order at large cannot be responsible for the deviance that occurs within it' (Connor, 1972, p. 242). Although soviet theory accepts that deviance is caused by social factors it rejects those basic 'societal' factors as possible causes, preferring to concentrate on 'middle-range' theories of defective socialization:

> Blame for deviance and the attitudes that foster it is internalized, but only at middle levels of the social structure, which cannot be controlled completely from the top, and 'externalized' in time and space to historical forces beyond effective control and to the machinations of a hostile capitalist world. . . . Thus, the responsibility for deviance is deflected from any potentially blameworthy properties of the society itself onto history and imperfect immediate environments.
> [Connor, 1972, p. 244]

A similar version of the soviet technique of 'disowning' deviance so as to avoid the need for closer scrutiny of their political and social arrangements, is one of the themes of the radical critiques of contemporary American and British criminology. The perspectives, methods and institutional bases of established criminology have served (wittingly or unwittingly) to deflect serious enquiry away from political and socio-economic structures, towards the middle-range areas of piece-meal social engineering in fields such as housing, community organization and education. We can only speculate upon the conclusions that might be reached if criminological attention were to be focused instead upon our major social institutions. An understanding of this aspect of criminology may be the first step towards a greater understanding of the criminogenic factors in society — bringing us back full circle to the conclusions reached by Lindesmith and Levin in their analysis of the Lombrosian myth:

> The progress of science is often portrayed as a majestic and inevitable evolution of ideas in a logical sequence of successively closer approximations to the truth. We have shown that this conception does not apply to criminology wherein myth and fashion and social conditions have often exercised an influence quite unrelated to the soundness of theories or to the implications of accumulated evidence. One of the sources of protection against invasion by fads, and against these extra-theoretical influences, of which criminology of today has not availed itself, is a sound appreciation of its own past.
> [Lindesmith and Levin, 1937b, p. 671]

CRIME RATES AND INDIVIDUAL BEHAVIOUR

One of the distinctions often made in surveys of criminological theories is between those which attempt to account for differences in the *comparative rates* and distribution of crime, between social groups or over time and space, and those theories which try to explain why *particular individuals* indulge in criminal behaviour. As the former tend to focus upon factors in the social environment and the latter upon physical or personality characteristics of the individual they are often referred to as sociological and psychological theories, respectively. Thus crime as a social fact is traditionally explained by social factors, whereas, crime as an individual fact tends to be explained by factors within the individual. Unfortunately this apparently neat dichotomy has sometimes resulted in a confusion of the separate issues involved. The question of the *level of explanation* (i.e. crime rates *v.* individual behaviour) needs to be kept strictly separate from that of the nature of

explanatory factors (i.e. societal influences *v.* personal characteristics). It is often better to avoid the use of generic labels such as
'sociological' or 'psychological' altogether, unless their use is
carefully specified and qualified in terms of the above distinctions.

Albert Cohen discussed this issue in *Deviance and Control,* but
even he failed to avoid a certain amount of confusion. Cohen
identified as the 'psychological level of explanation' that which
involves what he called 'kinds-of-people' theories, and typically
tries to answer the question 'What sort of person would do this sort
of thing?'. The 'sociological level of explanation', on the other hand,
concerns itself with the properties of the system and tries to provide
answers to the question 'What is it about social structures that
accounts for differences between them?' (Cohen, 1966, pp. 45-6).
There is no doubt that he was referring here to different levels of
explanation and not primarily to different kinds of explanatory
factors:

> We may call this level of enquiry *sociological.* We do not oppose
> sociological explanations to psychological explanations; they are
> not rival answers to the same questions, but answer different
> questions about the same sort of behaviour.
> [Cohen, 1966, p. 46]

It is unfortunate that in this key passage he refers so loosely to
'explanations', which could be interpreted as meaning explanatory
factors, and also refers to 'the same sort of behaviour' without
repeating his earlier distinction between crime as individual
behaviour and crime as a property of social systems. He then
proceeded to outline a more complicated view of the relationship
between the different levels of theory and the nature of explanatory
factors:

> Psychological theories have implications for the sociological
> level, and every sociological theory makes assumptions explicitly
> or implicitly, about the psychological level. . . . Psychological
> inquiry is concerned with identifying variables and processes
> involved in the motivation of deviance and conformity, and with
> constructing exact theories about their interrelationships. Socio-
> logical theory is concerned with identifying the variables and
> processes in the larger social system that in turn shape those that
> are involved in motivation, and that determine their distribution
> within the system.
> [Cohen, 1966, pp. 46-7]

He is now talking about 'psychological theory' and 'sociological theory', and even though the points he makes are most important he is raising issues that are related to, but separate from, sociological and psychological levels of explanation. Research and theory within each discipline can address itself to either level of explanation, hence the need to avoid unqualified use of the terms, which only adds to the confusion.

In practice, when we examine examples of particular theories, we find that similar confusion obtains regarding research methods and objectives. Most of the confusion is to be found within the theories of sociologists, as those who have analysed crime from a biological, psychiatric or psychological point of view have usually been in little doubt that their primary focus was upon explaining crime at the level of the individual offender. On the other hand, some of those involved in sociologically-oriented studies of crime have been less clear about their objectives, particularly as to whether they are exclusively concerned with the societal level of explanation for crime rates or whether they are also involved in discovering specifically social influences upon the behaviour of the individual. Two examples should help to illustrate the extent to which a critical awareness of these issues has existed, and at the same time shed some incidental light upon the implications (if any) for the long-standing dispute about the 'free-will' of the individual in his social environment.

The work of Adolphe Quetelet provides a good starting point. Quetelet was not just a pioneer in the study of official statistics, but also an ideal example of those sociologists of crime who are exclusively concerned with explaining trends and patterns of crime, as a social fact *par excellence.* In his case this concern was closely associated with a belief that crime rates were also to be explained exclusively in terms of social factors. Within this nexus of the socially determined social reality of crime, Quetelet was nevertheless able to leave room for the exercise of free-will.

The discovery for which Quetelet is mainly remembered was that of the 'constancy of crime'. This referred not only to the allegedly constant relationships between detected and undetected crime, and between crimes known to the police and the numbers of persons prosecuted (see Chapter 1), but to the more fundamental constancy and regularity in the number of crimes committed. This finding (originally published in his *Physique Sociale* of 1835) derived from an analysis of French crime statistics between 1826-30, and although he was later to recognize that this constancy held good only over relatively short periods of time during which there were no major changes in social conditions, it still remained at the centre of his theoretical interpretations of crime rates. According to van Bemmelen's analysis of Quetelet's ideas and work, the main reason that explained this essential regularity of crime was that man's social life (including, therefore, criminal behaviour) was governed by laws of nature which emanated from the innermost structure of a given society (van Bemmelen, 1952, pp. 219-20; for an English equivalent see Rawson, 1839). Quetelet took great pains to explain how these 'laws of nature' were compatible with the concept of individual free-will. He insisted that individuals could exercise a meaningful degree of choice in shaping the course of their lives, with some exceptional people being able to bring about change in society itself; but in the aggregate the effects of individual freedom of choice cancelled each other out, in a similar fashion to that which makes possible actuarial tables for insurance purposes. The overall effect of individual free-will upon social phenomena was thus seen to be constricted within narrow limits and described as 'an accidental cause'. The reception accorded to these rather idiosyncratic ideas was not enhanced by Quetelet's use of another misleading concept, that of *penchant au crime*, which can be roughly translated as 'criminal tendency'. It is not difficult to see why this term was misunderstood in Quetelet's own day, as if it was meant to specify the moral characteristics of individuals. In fact, *penchant au crime* was intended to indicate only the arithmetical probability of crimes being committed by people in certain social categories, just as Quetelet referred to the statistical likelihood of marriage as the *tendance au marriage* (van Bemmelen, 1952, pp. 222-3).

Thus we find in the ideas of Quetelet, as also of his contemporary Guerry, a consistent if at times rather abtruse set of sociological notions of the regularity of crime, which were seen to be consistent with individual free-will. The whole system was subject to a 'law of accidental causes' whereby 'man is subject to certain deviations from the average in regard to his moral qualities, just as he is in regard to his physical traits, and these fluctuations to which he is subject vary according to the general law of individual variation' (Quetelet, *Du Système Social*, 1848, p. 92, quoted by van Bemmelen, 1952, p. 224).

Just as Quetelet's emphasis on social explanation has often been seen as a denial of the commonsense notion of free-will, so with the rise of the urban sociologists' interest in crime in Chicago during the 1920s there has been a persistent tendency to interpret their findings in terms of 'geographical determinism'. Clifford Shaw and Henry McKay carried out detailed surveys of the patterns of the geographical distribution of crime commission and offender residence in many of the major cities of the United States. The 'constancy of crime' which they discovered was closely related to the existence of urban 'criminal areas' which were characterized by a wide range of indices of physical and social deterioration. It seemed obvious to many commentators, then as now, that there must be a simple cause-effect relationship whereby areas of poverty, poor housing, illness and immigrant population were direct breeding grounds of delinquency and crime. On the contrary, Terence Morris (1957) has clearly shown how a careful reading of Shaw and McKay proves that they at least entertained no such ideas of naive geographical or social determinism of deviant behaviour. In Shaw's first major study, *Delinquency Areas*, he quickly recognized the importance of individual attitudes in mediating the effects of the local environment and introduced 'situational analysis' to examine this vital process of interaction between the individual and his social world. Shaw spelled out his rejection of an easy deterministic view:

> It should be clearly understood that this study is not an attempt to show that delinquency is caused by the simple fact of location. We are pointing out here that delinquency tends to occur in a characteristic type of area. More intensive analysis of these areas is necessary before the factors that characterise delinquency-producing situations can be indicated.
> [Shaw, 1929, p. 21]

Despite the very tentative theoretical conclusions drawn by the author from these early studies, it was largely on the strength of them that the Chicago Area Project was inaugurated in 1932, to combat increasing crime and delinquency by fostering greater community involvement and organization to counteract the negative forces working towards deviant behaviour. In a later more comprehensive study Shaw and McKay reiterated that local conditions do not in themselves cause or explain delinquency:

> While these maps and statistical data are useful in locating different types of area, in differentiating the areas where the rates

of delinquency are high from areas where the rates are low, and in predicting or forecasting expected rates, they do not furnish an explanation of delinquent conduct.
[Shaw and McKay, 1969, p. 14]

Specific attention was drawn to the fact that *geographic areas do not in themselves produce delinquent children*, but delinquency appears to be a combined result of the failure of the normal processes of socialization and a breakdown of the machinery whereby the needs of the local population are met through community institutions. The authors emphasized the inherent limitations of much sociological research, in which *correlations* of environmental factors with criminal behaviour are often interpreted as *causal* associations (Shaw and McKay, 1969, pp. 384-7); but the work of the Chicago ecologists continues to be interpreted as providing explanations for urban crime at the individual level. In many other ways too the experience of Shaw and McKay sums up the typical dilemma of the sociologist as criminologist, in his personal and public capacities. The initial inclination of the academic may well be to emphasize the limited nature of his findings, but invariably other factors enter into the situation, including fellow academics who may be interested in the causes of crime at a different level and those in the wider community interested in understanding delinquency in order to control it.

Interest in the ecological approach to the study of crime has continued throughout the last half-century, although too often exhibiting some of the worst features of atheoretical statistical empiricism. Recently, however, in Britain there has been a revival of ecological work by urban geographers and criminologists which shows signs of a broader awareness of the theoretical limitations and potential of this method. The report of the first stage of the Sheffield Study on Urban Social Structure and Crime by Baldwin and Bottoms included a reassessment of the achievements of the Chicago school. In the authors' view ecological studies still have a contribution to make to the investigation of crime provided they are restricted to the two aspects of 'areal epidemiology' and detailed 'naturalistic descriptions' of urban neighbourhoods. They more clearly recognized what Shaw and McKay were intermittently aware of, that as far as explanations of delinquency are concerned the ecological approach can only provide signposts for further investigations and not any final answers:

If one breaks away from the tradition of regarding epidemiology and ecology as important *per se*, and regards them rather as important *means to an end*, the end being to provide explanations and meanings of the phenomena studied, then such work . . . can be regarded as crucial contributors. This in itself however implies a particular methodology: that one will begin with epidemiological variations as a first stage in research, and then in the second stage go on to investigate more deeply certain relationships discovered. [Baldwin and Bottoms, 1976, p. 16]

This raises questions of specific relevance to the objectives and interpretation of ecological studies, and also in a more general way directs attention to a closer scrutiny of the stated purposes and legitimate conclusions of a much wider range of criminological studies. Such an examination would reveal the limited nature of much research that attempts to explain crime; at the same time, it suggests that there is much more in common between sociological and psychological approaches than separates them, whether at the level of explanation or in terms of explanatory factors.

Finally, to understand a little better how the present situation has arisen we need to recognize the important role that *prediction* has played in criminological research and theory development. Neither the study of crime rates nor the analysis of individual criminal behaviour need necessarily be aimed at the discovery of causal relationships of any kind. Provided that the precise nature and objects of the exercise are made clear, useful purposes may be served by research which is aimed at the discovery of facts and associations which improve the identification, prediction or other manipulation of crime at the societal or individual levels. For example, ecological research may have been discredited in terms of many of its early claims and ambitions but may nevertheless serve a useful purpose in identifying those areas of cities which can be the subject of further investigation or targets for programmes of crime prevention and control. It is just as important to recognize that research which fails to provide an adequate explanation of crime can nevertheless be useful for other purposes, as it is to recognize that research which is able to predict crime (to some degree) has no necessary validity at the explanatory level. Whether concerned with attempts to forecast trends in crime rates or to discover the risk of a particular child becoming delinquent or a paroled prisoner committing a further offence, the predictive accuracy and validity of such studies need bear no relationship to their causal accuracy or explanatory value. This simple but important distinction tends to be overlooked or blurred in the process of conducting and interpreting criminological research. It is rare to find the clarity that is to be found in the English borstal prediction study of Mannheim and Wilkins who took great care to stress that the factors found to be related to the risks of a borstal trainee being reconvicted were not necessarily related to the causes of the criminal behaviour in question:

> There is no way of knowing whether the word 'cause' may or not be reasonably applied to any of our factors. We shall make no claim to unravel the causes of recidivism and we would not claim that even those factors which we find to be most highly associated with failure are in any part a cause of such failure.
> [Mannheim and Wilkins, 1955, pp. 43-4]

A common reason for the failure to acknowledge this essential difference is that many studies are concerned at one and the same time to unravel the factors which *explain* criminal behaviour, which *predict* it and which can be used for the *control* or *treatment* of crime. An example of the coalescing of multiple objectives in this way is the study by Sheldon and Eleanor Glueck (1950). Judging by the main theme of their introductory chapter, it appeared that their clear intention was to *discover the causes* of juvenile delinquency. However, on closer inspection it becomes obvious that a number of crucial decisions about the selection of the research samples and the characteristics to be investigated were justified solely in terms of the development of a social *prediction* table for identifying 'potential delinquents' at a pre-school age; further, the predictions were to be based on factors which could be manipulated to *prevent* delinquency. The authors' subsequent 'discovery' that the roots of delinquency lie in the 'under-the-roof' culture of family relationships could hardly be judged to be the result of a single-minded search for causal explanation.

The prediction of delinquency or recidivism as an objective in its own right has a definite place in criminology, provided that its limitations are acknowledged. Prediction of this sort has little bearing on the issue of individual freedom of choice, and even on its own terms the efficiency of statistical (or clinical) prediction in criminology is not very impressive (see Simon, 1971). The main lesson, for the present discussion, is the need to keep the issues of prediction and explanation more separate than has often been the case in the past, where the positivist 'package-deal' included explanation, prediction and prevention in one undifferentiated set of research objectives and interpretations.

MANY CAUSES OR MANY CRIMES?

Following the discrediting of early 'monolithic' theories of crime, based on assumptions of constitutional differences between criminals and non-criminals, and the apparent failure of more general sociological theories of crime to comprehend fully the intricacies of the social phenomenon of crime, two of the most popular directions taken were, firstly, the 'multi-factor' or 'multi-causal' approach and, secondly, the attempt to subdivide crime into a number of discrete categories. The former retained a belief in the homogeneity of crime but looked for a multiplicity of causes, whereas the latter substituted many different types of crime for the single concept.

Walker described the rise of multi-factor theories as follows:

> The assumption of multiple determination is neither a theory nor an anti-theory, but an hypothesis about theories. It suggests that nothing which can be regarded as a single variable will ever be found to explain, without exceptions, any group of delinquents or delinquent acts; and that only a theory formulated in terms of two or more variables has any prospect of doing so. Contrary to Wilkins' assertion (Wilkins, 1964, pp. 36-7) it is not untestable: it is tested every time a new monolith is erected and demolished. [Walker, 1966, p. 8]

A classic illustration is found in the work of the English criminologist Cyril Burt. In *The Young Delinquent*, Burt decisively rejected the traditionally narrow search for the causes of crime in some 'solitary panacea':

> One striking fact leaps out in bold relief — the fact of multiple determination. Crime is assignable to no single universal source, nor yet to two or three: it springs from a wide variety, and usually from a multiplicity of alternative and converging influences. . . . It needs many coats of pitch to paint a thing thoroughly black. The

nature of these factors, and of their varying combinations, differs
greatly from one individual to another.
[Burt, 1944, pp. 599-600]

In his research he was able to identify more than 170 distinct
factors each allegedly conducive to juvenile delinquency; and even
when his conclusions were restricted to the most influential factors
he was still able to describe as many as seventy different conditions
which formed, in one instance or another, the principal reason for a
child's offence — 'on an average, therefore, each delinquent child is
the product of nine or ten subversive circumstances, one as a rule
preponderating, and all conspiring to draw him into crime' (Burt,
1944, p. 602). As the term implies, theories of multiple determination
have normally been expressed in causal language, but Burt showed
some awareness of the potential misconceptions by acknowledging
the fact that most of the identified factors and conditions were not
found exclusively among delinquents: the incidence was much less
among non-delinquents (averaging three per case instead of nine or
ten) but nevertheless it meant that in the cases of some children of
the same social class 'identical conditions may coexist without
plunging them into a criminal career' (Burt, 1944, p. 602). Indeed,
Burt recognized that the true implications of criminological theories
were at the level of probability rather than total determination: 'It
must therefore, as a rule, be either the number of factors or the
particular combination of them, that renders delinquency a probable
result' (Burt, 1944, p. 602).

An equally well known example of a multi-factor approach is that
of the Gluecks, to which a number of references have already been
made. They proclaimed the need for what they described as 'an
eclectic approach to the study of the causal process in human
motivation and behaviour . . . designed to reveal meaningful
integrations of diverse data from several levels of enquiry' (Glueck
and Glueck, 1950, p. 7). Their painstaking project investigated an
enormous range of factors and conditions, although, as we have
seen, their methodology was biased against certain socio-cultural
and environmental factors. The initial theoretical focus was upon
the mechanism of multiple determination, with the intention of
highlighting the selectivity and interaction occurring at 'the point of
contact between specific social and biologic processes as they
coalesce, accommodate, or conflict in individuals' (Glueck and

Glueck, 1950, p. 7). Despite this, their eventual conclusions reflected more conventional thinking:

> The separate findings, independently gathered, integrate into a dynamic pattern which is neither exclusively biologic nor exclusively socio-cultural, but which derives from an interplay of somatic, temperamental, intellectual, and socio-cultural forces. [Glueck and Glueck, 1950, p. 281]

Nevertheless there were hints of the way the Gluecks' thinking was to develop in later years towards the typological approach to delinquency. They recognized that some of the differentiating characteristics involved the majority of delinquents but others fewer, so that 'the variety of these traits and the fact that some of them do not usually accompany others suggest that the delinquent group is a composite of several sub-types' (Glueck and Glueck, 1950, p. 275). Their support for a 'multi-dimensional' interpretation seems to have been an attempt to overcome the perceived deficiencies of single-factor analysis inasmuch as they realized that in the general community most boys with particular characteristics did *not* become delinquents. It would seem that they introduced multiple determination because of a belief that it provided a causal link qualitatively different from the statistical probability derivable from single factors:

> If, however, we take into account the dynamic interplay of these various levels and channels of influence, a tentative causal formula or law emerged, which tends to accommodate these puzzling divergencies so far as the great mass of delinquents is concerned. [Glueck and Glueck, 1950, p. 281]

It is difficult to see how, using the methodology adopted by the Gluecks, the mere combination of factors related to the future probability of delinquency can radically alter the nature of the relationships suggested by the data. The more appropriate conclusion to be drawn is that whether the effects of single factors or multiple factors are analysed in this way the result can only be expressed in terms of an increased or reduced likelihood of delinquent behaviour.

In a later paper, Sheldon Glueck elaborated upon his view of the multi-causal dynamics of delinquency and crime. He suggested that the same sort of criminal behaviour could be the result of a *variety* of 'causal syndromes', in the sense that in one case biological and in another case socio-cultural factors could exert most influence in the interplay of internal and external forces leading to deviant behaviour (Glueck, 1956, p. 105). In place of any single specific theory or causal factor 'inevitably and always conducing to delinquency' he wished to substitute a conception of the *interchangeability* of aetiological traits and factors as the basis for a realistic and relatively accurate doctrine of causation:

> Any of these factors alone or in various combinations may or may not bring about delinquency, depending on the balance of energy tendencies at a particular time, in the particular individual involved. . . . This is a realistic conception of causation, for by isolating the biosocial syndromes most usually operative in the lives of delinquents and most usually absent in the lives of non-delinquents, it not only adds to understanding of cause and effect but it highlights the traits, factors and areas most relevant to prediction, to therapeutic effort in the individual case and to prophylactic effort in general.
> [Glueck, 1956, pp. 105-6]

Despite the greater conceptual complexity, and the important recognition that different causes can bring about the same effect, the essential message seems unchanged. The concepts of interchangeability and differential weighting of factors can simply be seen as descriptions of the elements of statistical probability, which need have no implications for causes, but may be entirely relevant for other purposes such as prediction and social intervention.

Two recent English studies of delinquency can serve as final illustrations of multi-factor approaches; their significance lies not only in the fact that they were based on measures of self-reported as well as officially known delinquency but that they showed a greater (if sporadic) awareness of the nature and even the limitations of the exercise in which they were involved.

West and Farrington investigated the long-term development of delinquency in a sample of 400 schoolboys selected at the age of eight and studied closely for more than ten years (West and Farrington, 1969, 1973, 1977). The range of factors investigated was typical of the wide-ranging strategy of multi-factor approaches, with the longitudinal method lending itself well to the investigation of changes over time in attitudes and behaviour. The authors were careful to acknowledge the limitations of statistical correlation and modestly disclaimed having discovered the causes of delinquency:

A statistical correlation does not necessarily imply a direct causal link, and the statistical importance of these five background factors does not mean that they were the essential causes of delinquency.... No amount of statistical analysis of correlations discovered in social surveys is likely to succeed in showing conclusively which particular elements are most to blame. It seems difficult to get beyond the observation that certain adversities are linked with delinquency and that an accumulation of these adversities makes a delinquent outcome more probable.
[West and Farrington, 1973, p. 191]

Their substantive conclusions were couched in terms of the ability of certain factors to distinguish those boys 'at greater risk'. Five background factors were of particular significance in picking out those who were much more likely than average to become delinquent, viz. low family income, large family size, parental criminality, low intelligence and poor parental behaviour. The boys affected by these five adverse background features were 'rendered extremely vulnerable to delinquency', so that, of the 63 boys who had three or more such factors, half became juvenile delinquents (West and Farrington, 1973, p. 190). In terms of predictability these factors were as efficient as the Social Prediction Scale developed by the Gluecks, but even so the boys predicted as 'most vulnerable' still stood a better-than-evens chance of *not* becoming delinquent, and the majority of future delinquents did *not* come from those small groups identified as vulnerable.

After their bold disclaimer of being unable to go beyond observations that certain adversities seem to make delinquency 'more probable', something of a jarring note occurs towards the end of their study when they make a special plea on behalf of the multi-causal approach:

The Cambridge Study in Delinquent Development suggests that delinquency arises from a complex interaction between the individual home atmosphere, the personal qualities of the boy and the circumstances in which the family live. However unfashionable or inconvenient, a multi-causal theoretical approach seems necessary.
[West and Farrington, 1973, p. 201]

It would have been more consistent to have retained the caution of their earlier statements, and while accepting the important *indicative* nature of the identified factors to have re-emphasized the risk of drawing *causal* conclusions from this kind of survey data alone.

The final example for brief mention is the survey of 1,400 London schoolboys by William A. Belson, *Juvenile Theft: the Causal Factors.* This research project was specially commissioned to investigate *causal factors* and therefore the shape of the final report was dictated (and at times distorted) by the setting out of the findings in terms of the systematic testing of numerous hypotheses and their corollaries. Belson nailed his colours to the mast of multiple causation in the very opening sections of the report. He rejected the idea of any single factor being hypothesized as a sole cause of juvenile stealing, and stated that 'throughout, the basic assumption has been one of multiple causality' (Belson, 1975, p. vi). He left the reader in no doubt whatsoever that *causality* was being postulated, despite the admitted unfashionability of this stance among criminologists which he thought might be partly attributable to the mistaken view that a causal approach implies a single cause. Belson not only attempted to liberate the idea of causality from the monolithic approach to theories of crime, but he was equally concerned to liberate the multi-causal concept from any kind of predictable dynamic that strictly determines subsequent behaviour:

> The approach to causality adopted here is *multiple* in character. It is multiple in the sense that the specific variable named in the hypotheses as causal . . . were from the outset regarded as no more than contributory in character. . . . It was also fully recognised that there is likely to be complex interaction between the different factors that turn out to be contributory.
> [Belson, 1975, p. 3]

The potential value of this study lay in its single-minded objective in causal terms, which shaped the research strategy and data analysis throughout. If the methodology had been adequate to the task, a major breakthrough might have occurred in the history of multi-factor theories of crime. As it is serious doubts exist about the methodology (Sethi, 1976) and so that breakthrough is yet to come.

Albert Cohen described the multi-factor approach as 'an abdication of the quest for a theory', inasmuch as it claims that one particular crime is 'caused' by a certain combination of factors and another crime by a different combination (Cohen, 1951). Similarly, Leslie Wilkins refused to dignify it by the term theory, on the grounds that it leads to no testable hypothesis or practical consequences that are of any use; he concluded that 'at best it could be considered an anti-theory which proposes that no theory can be formed regarding crime' (Wilkins, 1964, p. 37). Both these criticisms are more justified if seen as attacks on the eclectic version whereby different crimes are attributed to different (but often single and separate) causes. They are much less relevant in terms of some of the classic multiple-causation studies that have been carried out. At the source of some of the misplaced criticism lies the issue of how far multiple-factor approaches can lay claim not only to be reckoned as theories, but to provide any kind of 'scientific explanation' of criminal behaviour. Cohen, for example, clearly stated that in his view an adequate explanation need not be restricted to just a single factor but required 'a single theory or system of theory applicable to all cases' (Cohen, 1951). Similarly, Sutherland and Cressey joined in the attack on those multi-factor theorists who indulged in dubious eclecticism, and whose position was based upon a confusion of single-factor explanations and single unified theories of criminality. In their view 'neither a statement of one fact ("single factor") nor a series of such statements ("multiple factors") about crime is a theoretical explanation'; what is required is a single theory which organizes and relates the variables, whatever their number:

> If criminology is to be scientific, the heterogeneous collection of 'multiple factors' known to be associated with crime and criminality should be organized and integrated by means of an explanatory theory which has the same characteristics as the scientific explanations in other fields of study. That is, the conditions which are said to cause crime should always be present when crime is present and they should always be absent when crime is absent.
> [Sutherland and Cressey, 1970, p. 72]

These criticisms go beyond the issue of multi-causality into the fundamental expectations and conceptions of explanation in criminology discussed in the final section of this chapter. But first consider the second main response of criminologists to the apparently fruitless search for the 'criminologist's stone', namely that version of eclecticism which seeks a different cause for different kinds of crime, and which has led to the development of criminological typologies.

Classification of crime and criminals has been a feature of criminology since its pioneering days, and although typologies have been developed for legal, administrative and penological purposes, as well as aetiological, their achievements in these other fields will not be our main concern here. It is now accepted as a criminological platitude that, as Vold phrased it:

> Crime must be recognized clearly as not being a unitary phenomenon but as consisting of many kinds of behaviour occurring under many different situations. No single theory therefore should be expected to provide the explanations for the many varieties of behavior involved.
> [Vold, 1958, pp. 313-14]

Sutherland expressed similar sentiments nearly twenty years before when he concluded that 'in order to make progress in the explanation of crime, it is desirable to break crime into more homogeneous units' (Sutherland, 1939). There has been much less agreement on the basis upon which crime and criminals ought to be classified for aetiological purposes. A number of basic distinctions have usually been drawn in the literature on criminal typologies (see, for example, Gibbons, 1965, 1975; Ferdinand, 1966; Roebuck, 1967; Bottoms, 1973; Clinard and Quinney, 1973; Hood and Sparks, 1970).

A common approach is to distinguish between types of *offender* and types of *offence*, but this has given rise to some confusion so that I prefer to use the terms suggested by Gibbons (1975), with classifications based on: (1) *personality types* (amongst offenders); (2) *patterns of offenders* (according to their criminal behaviour); and (3) *patterns of crime* (events). In this way it is easier to recognize the fact that many so-called 'offence typologies' are really *patterns of offenders*, and also, as Gibbons pointed out, that there are very few true typologies of *crime patterns* in their own right.

A second important distinction relates to the way in which typologies are constructed. Hood and Sparks have distinguished between those constructed by *empirical* and those by *theoretical* methods. Empirical typologies start with observed patterns of criminal behaviour and group together those individuals or behaviour patterns that appear to share relevant features, clearly distinguishing one category from another; because it is firmly grounded in observed data Hood and Sparks suggest this could be called the 'look and see' method of classification (Hood and Sparks, 1970, p. 117). In contrast, theoretical typologies start with a theory from which is deduced a relatively specific basis for classification; the criteria for grouping individuals or behaviour are those which seem relevant to the pre-selected theoretical framework — but they may not in fact correspond closely to anything discoverable in the real world of criminal behaviour. In practice it is rare to find pure examples of either kind of typology as few empirical ones are totally devoid of some theoretical preconceptions and most theoretical typologies are based on some expectations regarding the likely fit between observed data and theoretical requirements.

Classifications of offenders according to their personality types are of limited value in explaining or predicting criminal behaviour. They have usually been developed by psychiatrists or psychologists, as attempts to explain crime at the individual level. They may be theoretical typologies, such as that of Friedlander (1947) based on Freudian theory, or derived from the empirical study of delinquents, of which perhaps the best known example is that of Hewitt and Jenkins (1946; see also Gibbens, 1963). Many of them share the characteristic of multi-factor approaches, in that they classify and subdivide offenders into different personality types, but treat the category of criminal behaviour to be explained as indivisible. Hewitt and Jenkins are exceptions, as they claimed to find specific types of crime behaviour related to specific personality syndromes, although a replication study of English approved school boys failed to confirm the relationships (Field, 1967). The two usual weaknesses of personality typologies are that most of them suffer from the strategic limitation of being *retrospective* studies of the early childhood development of convicted delinquents; secondly, their common basis in personality theory and treatment objectives severely limits their contribution to the understanding of the causes of crime as such. They are very obvious candidates for Matza's criticism of 'overprediction' and an 'embarrassment of riches', given the likelihood that most of the non-delinquent population can also be allocated to one or other of the proposed categories. Hood and Sparks summarized their weaknesses:

> The majority of typologies of this kind have not been related to any kind of criminological theory. . . . Instead, they are what might be called typologies of *persons* — they classify human beings according to attributes such as personality or character traits or social background, which apply to human beings generally and not just to offenders. . . . They take no account of different forms of criminal or deviant behaviour . . . with the result that they cannot explain why certain personal characteristics lead to violent crime in some cases and purposive theft in others. . . . Moreover, they cannot explain why those personal

characteristics should lead to any kind of crime in some cases but not in others.
[Hood and Sparks, 1970, p. 128]

Typologies based on patterns of offenders, according to their criminal behaviour, manage to satisfy a number of these objections. They are usually related directly or indirectly to a specific theory of crime, and their main aim is to identify as many as possible of the theoretically relevant subdivisions of crime, each with its own set of explanatory factors. The empirically constructed typologies of this kind, however, are equally retrospective and run the risk of 'explaining' more crime than actually occurs. Most of them are derived from sociological perspectives on crime, but can be directed at explanations at either the individual or societal level. Many of these sociological typologies may appear (and claim) to be offence typologies, but if Gibbons' distinction is kept in mind it will be seen that the vast majority are based on the *grouping of offenders,* according to their offence pattern. An example of this sort of confusion is the typology of 'criminal behaviour systems' developed by Clinard and Quinney (1973), in which they identified nine variations: violent personal, occasional property, public order, conventional, political, occupational, corporate, organized and professional crime. Each criminal behaviour system was characterized along five 'theoretical dimensions', relating to legal aspects, criminal career, group support, correspondence between criminal and legitimate behaviour, and societal reaction and legal processing. Although this is often described as an offence typology, in its fundamental objectives and construction it is clearly an offender typology, with the variable dimensions always being focused on the offender. Clinard and Quinney clarified their intentions:

A *criminal behavior system* could be constructed that would consider all three areas of phenomena associated with crime viz. criminal law, individual behaviour, social reaction. Such a typology would suggest how persons with certain characteristics and behaviors develop patterns that have a certain probability of becoming defined as criminal and receive a particular reaction from society. The development of a multidimensional and integrative typology is our primary concern.
[Clinard and Quinney, 1973, p. 13]

This scheme is subject to the criticism that can be levelled at most other offender typologies, namely that most offenders do not fit neatly into any single offence type. The categories are often very broad indeed, whether considered from the legal, situational or sociological point of view, so they are unlikely to have very many meaningful features in common for aetiological purposes.

At the other end of the spectrum, there is the empirical 'legalistic' typology of Roebuck (1967), based on the known arrest records of offenders and varying from 'single pattern type' (only ever arrested for one kind of crime), through double and triple patterns, to 'mixed pattern' (or 'jack-of-all-trades') and no pattern at all. Its method of construction and conceptual framework ensured some correspondence with social reality, but its theoretical expectations seemed very optimistic in view of the notorious lack of agreement between legal labels and actual behavioural categories. Only a minority (37 per cent) of Roebuck's original sample were of the single pattern type. Nevertheless Roebuck claimed to have found significant differences in the social and psychological background factors of offenders with different arrest patterns and was convinced that 'the aetiological process that leads to one kind of criminal career differs from that which leads to another' (Roebuck, 1967, p. 16). His theoretical assumptions were an unusual mixture of traditional and more radical ideas: he eschewed the idea of any adequate general theory of crime, but believed in the necessity of an inter-disciplinary approach to typology, leading back to the conclusion that criminal behaviour results from multiple causation (!) (Roebuck, 1967, p.16).

One of the most satisfactory of the attempts to construct aetiological typologies is the work of Don C. Gibbons (1965). The derivation of his classification of juvenile delinquents and adult offenders was more theoretical than empirical, centred round the concept of 'role-career'. Gibbons identified fifteen adult criminal role-career types, each of which had separate specifications ('definitional dimensions') relating to offence behaviour, interactional setting, self-image and attitudes; finally, a number of background characteristics were hypothesized as being correlated with each type. The full list of adult types was:

1.   Professional thief
2.   Professional 'heavy' criminal
3.   Semiprofessional property criminal
4.   Property offender — 'one-time loser'
5.   Automobile thief — 'joyrider'

6. Naive cheque forger
7. White-collar criminal
8. Professional 'fringe' violator
9. Embezzler
10. Personal offender — 'one-time loser'
11. 'Psychopathic' assaultist
12. Violent sex offender
13. Non-violent sex offender — 'rape'
14. Non-violent sex offender — statutory rape
15. Narcotic addict — heroin

Although this is admittedly not a fully comprehensive typology, but 'a reasonable middle ground between gross systems of differentiation among offenders . . . and categorical systems which employ an extremely large number of types' (Gibbons, 1965, p. 100), it too suffers from an inadequate empirical base, resulting in overlaps between some categories of offence behaviour and an over-differentiation within others that hardly seems justifiable. Neverthe-less, with modifications it does suggest a possible way forward along lines similar to those suggested in a review of classification methods by Bottoms (1973). In the first place, there is no reason why typologies should try to cover all possible criminal types *ab initio* — the 'ideal' of comprehensiveness seems to be reimporting 'general theory' notions into schemes that were meant to reflect a very different approach. Furthermore, there needs to be a closer relationship between theory and empiricism in the development of typologies, and here the model provided by 'grounded theory' seems particularly appropriate (Glaser and Strauss, 1967; Bottoms, 1973, pp. 32-45). In the last analysis, however, the very nature and complexity of criminal behaviour and its motivation may be the main stumbling-block to progress.

A recent personal reassessment of typological research by Gibbons reflected a major shift in his thinking, according to which the prospects for career-oriented typologies were not very bright as 'no fully comprehensive offender typology which subsumes most criminality within it yet exists' (Gibbons, 1975, p. 152). He believed that if a typology were ever to be constructed that did justice to the 'richness and variability' of offender behaviour the scheme would be so elegant and yet so complex that it would almost certainly frustrate any effort at causal analysis. There seemed little empirical support for the existence of the patterns and regularity of criminal behaviour assumed to exist, in one way or another, by all typologies:

> The notion of identifiable careers in criminality may be an
> hypothesis about behaviour which is too clinical. . . . Instead, it
> may be that many lawbreakers exhibit relatively unique com-
> binations of criminal conduct and attitudinal patterns. . . . The
> regularity and patterning assumed to characterise lawbreaking
> may not exist. The real world may stubbornly resist our efforts to
> simplify it by means of offender typologies.
> [Gibbons, 1975, pp. 152-3]

At this stage then we are forced to the conclusion that the multi-
factor and typological strategies in the study of crime causation are
too rooted in old ways of thinking to offer much hope of any
dramatic progress. Multi-causal approaches give too little attention
to what they are explaining and assume too much about the
explanatory significance of their favoured methodology, which can
rarely go beyond weak associations and limited predictions.
Typologists have too often wanted to run before they could walk, in
terms of developing full-blown classifications of all possible crimes
and criminals. Too many still see the exercise as a means towards
devising a general theory of crime, and there is too little awareness
of the primacy of theories being grounded in the evidence of the
real world of crime patterns. There will probably always be room
for understanding some crimes and some offenders by means of
identifying common 'role-careers' and so on, but for the rest we
must be content with rather more modest objectives.

EXPLANATION: THE OBJECTS OF THE EXERCISE

Having surveyed some of the paths and byways traversed by
criminologists in their search for the causes of crime, we must now
attempt to disentangle the various underlying conceptions and
expectations of explanations that have been partly to blame for the
confusion and lack of real progress. Theoretical criminology has
suffered badly from its neglect of certain fundamental issues in the
philosophy of social science, and it is hoped that the availability of
some good introductory texts (e.g. Ryan, 1970; Lessnoff, 1974;
Ford, 1975) as well as the brave essays within traditional criminology

by Nigel Walker (see, most recently, 1977) will help to make this aspect of their subject a more central concern for criminologists of all persuasions.

In view of the particular stimulus provided by radical criminology, it is fitting to begin with David Matza's (1964) incisive critique of the objectives and assumptions of positive criminology. A major feature of its quest for scientific status, according to Matza, was an image of man as fundamentally constrained, with criminal behaviour *determined* by a range of specified factors that differentiate the criminal from the non-criminal member of society.

Matza described this feature of traditional criminological theories as 'hard determinism' in contrast to the 'soft determinism' said to characterize mainstream sociology. The basic assertion of 'soft determinism' was that human actions are not deprived of freedom by virtue of being causally determined (Matza, 1964, p. 9). Although this critique had a deserved impact upon criminology and the sociology of deviance, it is clear that Matza was exercising a 'propagandist's licence' to caricature the nature and assumptions of much traditional theorizing within criminology, in order to drive home his message and prepare the ground for his alternative conception of 'delinquent drift'. He also failed to distinguish adequately between those theories which were aimed at explaining delinquency at the social or group level and those concerned with the behaviour of individuals. We have seen that the implications of the former for actually determining an individual's behaviour are strictly limited, and consequently some of Matza's criticisms on this score were misplaced. Nevertheless, his distinction between hard and soft determinism was a useful reminder of the overambitious claims that can undoubtedly be found within criminology. Just as the early sociologists of crime like Guerry and Quetelet claimed to have discovered 'laws of nature' to explain the regular patterns of crime, so later positivists, up to and including Professor Eysenck (1977), have often expounded their theories in terms predicated upon an extremely deterministic view of man. This must be accepted as a significant, albeit regrettable, element in the development of the subject, but hopefully it should not now be necessary to spend any time on disproving the extreme version of 'hard determinism'. Instead we shall concentrate on the interpretation and implications for criminological explanation of a version of 'soft determinism', as sketched by Matza and elaborated by Walker in his earliest discussion of the role of notions of 'probability' in sociological and psychological theories of crime:

> The sociologist's subculture or peer-group is just as much of a theoretical construct as the psychologist's type. . . . Now that most psychologists no longer attempt to explain the inevitability of delinquency in this or that individual, but are content to assign him to a type which is merely very likely to behave delinquently, another logical difference between their object-of-explanation and those of the sociologist has disappeared. . . . Both subcultural theory and psychological typologies are based on probability-groups, and thus belong to what Matza calls the 'soft determinism' with which the social sciences must be contented.
> [Walker, 1966, p. 14]

However timely may have been this recognition of similarity in the study of crime by sociologists and psychologists, neither Matza's 'soft determinism' nor Walker's stress upon 'probability groups' entirely comes to grips with some of the wider problems of explanation in the social sciences.

It is necessary at the outset to banish the spectre of 'scientific' explanation that still haunts the criminological scene. We agree with Walker that 'the assumption that the ideal explanation is scientific in form is out of date' (Walker, 1977, p. 140). It is arguable that criminologists' concern with the canons of scientific explanation over the years has blinded them to other more appropriate forms of explanation. In particular, we have seen how two of the character-istic objectives of explanation in science, *prediction* and *control*, have been central aspects of positivist criminology with its strongly 'correctional' bias; indeed, the achievements of many sociological studies of rates of crime have been limited to discoveries that serve purposes of prediction and control alone. Similarly, sociological and psychological studies of individual criminal behaviour, typically based on a multi-causal approach of a probabilistic kind, have usually only produced conclusions that are valid for predictive or treatment purposes. There can, of course, be much of value in theories which enable crime to be thus predicted, controlled or treated, but this is not the same as explanation, and progress on both fronts is likely to be that much greater if there is a clearer recognition of the different objectives involved.

Probabilistic 'explanations' and 'soft determinism' illustrate the inadequacies of the scientific model for explaining crime, and at the same time lack the potential strength of that model shown in the universal-mechanistic assumptions of 'hard determinism'. In drawing a distinction between what he called 'deductive-nomological' (D) and 'inductive-statistical' explanation Carl Hempel (1965, 1966) made clear that both were dependent upon the existence of general laws:

> Thus, probabilistic explanation, just like explanation in the manner of schema (D), is nomological in that it presupposes general laws, but because these laws are of statistical rather than of strictly universal form, the resulting explanatory arguments are inductive rather than deductive in character.
> [Hempel, 1966, p. 102]

The problem for criminology and the social sciences in general is that existing 'general laws' about behaviour tend to be strictly limited, and rarely provide firm ground for the *causal explanation* of human actions. Max Weber elaborated upon the dual nature of the explanatory task facing sociology, starting from his most famous dictum that the prime objective of sociological analysis is 'the interpretation of action in terms of its subjective meaning' (Weber, 1964, p. 94). Such interpretation of action involves above all a 'rational understanding of motivation':

> Thus, for a science which is concerned with the subjective meaning of action, explanation requires a grasp of the complex of meaning in which an actual course of understandable action thus interpreted belongs.
> [Weber, 1964, p. 96]

In their enthusiastic reception of Weber's key concept of 'understanding' (*verstehen*) sociologists and radical criminologists have often failed to represent adequately Weber's fuller views, with his stress on *explanatory* understanding and the need for explanations to be *causally adequate* as well as 'adequate at the level of meaning':

> Every interpretation attempts to attain clarity and certainty, but no matter how clear an interpretation as such appears to be from the point of view of meaning, it cannot on this account alone claim to be the causally valid interpretation. On this level it must remain only a peculiarly plausible hypothesis.
> [Weber, 1964, p. 96]

For the interpretation of a sequence of events to be called 'causally adequate', Weber meant that it had to be based on 'established generalizations from experience', so that there was a probability that it would always actually occur in the same way. It was just as essential for a correct causal interpretation to be adequate at the level of meaning as it was for it to be causally adequate:

> If adequacy in respect to meaning is lacking, then no matter how high the degree of uniformity and how precisely its probability can be numerically determined, it is still an incomprehensible statistical probability, whether dealing with overt or subjective processes. . . . Statistical uniformities constitute understandable types of action in the sense of this discussion, and thus constitute 'sociological generalizations', only when they can be regarded as manifestations of the understandable subjective meaning of a course of social action.
> [Weber, 1964, pp. 99-100]

We need look no further than this for a concise summary of the weaknesses of so many criminological theories, based on statistical correlations and content with their limited ability to predict rather than explain. Where we must begin to take issue with Weber is in his conception and interpretation of the requirements of 'causal adequacy'. Here he approached close to the mainstream of 'scientific explanation' in so far as he demanded that action should be related to *generalizations* and *predictive probability*:

> Thus causal explanation depends on being able to determine that there is a probability, which in the rare ideal case can be numerically stated, but is always in some sense calculable, that a given observable event (overt or subjective) will be followed or accompanied by another event. . . . Even the most perfect adequacy on the level of meaning has causal significance from a sociological point of view only in so far as there is some kind of proof for the existence of a probability that action in fact normally takes the course which has been held to be meaningful.
> [Weber, 1964, pp. 99-100]

It is now being increasingly recognized that in the field of human behaviour 'causal significance' and 'explanation' need not be confined to the restrictions imposed by the perceived canons of science. Just as Hempel recognized that, apart from a primary desire to control nature, equal motivation for scientific enquiry derived from 'man's insatiable intellectual curiosity, his deep concern to *know* the world he lives in, and to *explain,* and thus to *understand*' (Hempel, 1966, p. 95), so the social sciences must come to realize that the satisfaction of intellectual curiosity by the rendering intelligible of human action provides an explanation that is equally valid and sometimes more appropriate than the pursuit of more ambitious objectives.

Walker's (1977) recognition of these changing expectations for criminology led him to an interesting consideration of types of explanation found in historical analysis, and discussed in the writings of W.H. Dray (1957) and Hart and Honoré (1959). In particular, he noted the relevance of Dray's distinction between explanations of the 'why-necessarily?' and 'how-possibly?' types; in Walker's view these ideas suggest that to the extent that there exists a gap left by the discrediting of 'probability-explanations' this might usefully be filled by 'possibility-explanations' based on narrative accounts which satisfy the intellectual curiosity of the enquirer. I would wish to go further than, and yet in another sense not so far as, Walker in considering the potential value of 'possibility-explanations'; but first examine the relationship between them and various meanings of the term 'understanding' that are current within contemporary criminology.

One element in the persuasive use of the term 'understanding' is the way it is viewed as something opposed to a more scientific-mechanistic view of social behaviour. It shares a halo of meaning with concepts such as 'empathy' and 'appreciation' — which Matza has formulated in a special sense in contrast with traditional 'correctionalism' (Matza, 1969, pp. 15-40). It epitomizes the new 'subjectivism' as opposed to the old 'objective positivism'. Hempel's comments on the role of 'empathic understanding' in history show how it can be incorporated into a more conventional frame of reference, whereby it serves mainly as a heuristic device to suggest psychological hypotheses as possible explanatory principles for what is under investigation. As a research procedure, however, it cannot guarantee the soundness of any explanation to which it might lead, because this, according to Hempel, depends on the correctness of the underlying generalizations (Hempel, 1965, pp. 239-40). He used very similar arguments in his discussion of what he termed 'explanation sketches', which on the surface might appear to fulfil the same functions as the narrative accounts in possibility-explanations; but he made it absolutely clear that any superficial similarities were due to a misconception. Although an 'explanation sketch' would normally consist of a description of a connected sequence of events leading up to the action to be explained, it needed supplementation to be able to be regarded as a fully-fledged explanation, based on further empirical research in the directions suggested by the sketch; without this it was merely a 'pseudo-explanation sketch' (Hempel, 1965, p. 238).

An important feature of the 'understanding' that may be provided and the intellectual curiosity that may be satisfied by a convincing narrative account (or possibility-explanation) is that it usually refers to a particular case and one that has been studied in retrospect. Hart and Honoré pointed out that this is the commonest circumstance in which lawyers and historians are required to explain actions or events, and in this it is like many situations in everyday life that call for answers to the question 'why did so-and-so do that?':

> The lawyer and the historian are both primarily concerned to make causal statements about *particulars*. . . . Their characteristic concern with causation is not to discover connexions between types of events, and so not to *formulate* laws or generalizations, but is often to *apply* generalizations . . . to particular concrete cases.
> [Hart and Honoré, 1959, pp. 8-9]

Although the authors were aware of the need for such 'particular explanations' to rely on generalizations, of the kind Hempel believed were their vital ingredient, they did not believe that such explanations were in any sense *reducible* to such generalizations, and saw the need for considerations of a very different kind concerning the way in which generalizations may be combined and applied in particular cases (Hart and Honoré, 1959, p. 12). Hart and Honoré were absolutely right to stress the difference between the causal demands in a retrospective explanatory situation and those in a prospective predictive situation:

> It is, however, vital to see that logically the demands of the situation in which we ask for the cause of what has happened, and that in which we are concerned to predict are very different. In the first case it is an *inquest* that we are conducting. The 'effect' has happened.
> [Hart and Honoré, 1959, p. 43]

Prediction, as we have seen in criminology, requires a degree of certainty without necessarily any explanatory force, whereas explanation requires a degree of plausibility and adequacy at the level of meaning without necessarily any predictive power at all. Hence arises another typical dilemma of criminology, which is often concerned to explain *and* predict (both at the general and particular levels) and is unwilling or unable to separate the two tasks.

What conclusions emerge from this brief look at the problems of explanation in social science?

If we put aside any ideals of scientific explanation that might still be entertained, we reach a position that simply requires satisfactory *retrospective explanations* of particular cases or groups of cases. These explanations should be judged primarily according to the extent to which they render intelligible the behaviour under examination, with an intelligibility that is compatible with the subjective meaning of the behaviour for the actor(s) involved. The analysis of motivation and reasons plays a central part in the elucidation of subjective meaning. Except in a most indirect sense, adequate explanations of social action need not depend on (or derive from) any empirical generalizations; as Lessnoff puts it — 'how men generally behave in given types of situation may suggest a hypothesis for the explanation of an action, but cannot be conclusive as to its truth or falsity' (Lessnoff, 1974, p. 85). Indeed, in the explanation of deviant behaviour it is often the very lack of any correspondence with generalizable behaviour that is what has to be explained! Explanations neither depend on generalizations nor need they produce generalizations about future behaviour: 'What is decisive is that the explanation does *not* imply that if the same circumstances occurred on another occasion the man would act similarly' (Lessnoff, 1974, p. 88).

Ultimately, therefore, criminology along with the other social sciences has to take the basic explanatory task much more seriously than experimental science just because there are no consequential predictions to act as tests; explanations stand on their own in backward-looking isolation, with their major test being in the essential plausibility and rendering intelligible of the behaviour in question, both at the level of subjective meaning and compatability with any relevant features of the background situation. The vital contribution of reasons and motivation in this process does not mean a surrender to total subjectivism, as even Weber recognized that 'the "conscious motives" may well, even to the actor himself, conceal the various "motives" and "repressions" which constitute the real driving force of his action' (Weber, 1964, p. 97); the role of motives in explaining human behaviour confirms that the main purpose is one of satisfying intellectual curiosity:

A motive explains an action, not through subsumption under a
regular conjunction, much less through showing it to be inevitable,
but through rendering it *intelligible*.
[Lessnoff, 1974, p. 91]

To what extent, therefore, can trends be identified in contemporary criminology that seem to be pointing roughly in the right
direction?

Approaches to deviant behaviour that emphasize the importance
of *interaction* (between the actor and his situation) and *process*
would appear to share many of the assumptions about social
behaviour that make predictive explanation implausible or impossible. The extent to which the advocates of such approaches
accept the limitations that seem to flow from their assumptions
varies. In his discussion of theories that attempt to explain behaviour
at the individual level, Cohen moved from those which emphasize
the role of the actor, through those which emphasize the role of
situational factors, to theories that attempt to integrate the two
elements by emphasizing the interaction process, whereby 'the
deviant act develops over time through a series of stages' (Cohen,
1966, p. 44). He expressed this process diagrammatically in the form
of a 'tree' chart where many different branches flow from a single
trunk. The precise course of action which eventually results in a
deviant act is not fully determined by the initial state of affairs, but
resembles 'a tentative, groping, feeling-out process, never fully
determined by the past alone but always capable of changing its
course in response to changes in the current scene' (Cohen, 1966, p.
45). Despite the natural interpretation suggested by this imagery of
the essential unpredictability of this process, Cohen attempted to
preserve a modified version of prediction by claiming that the
pathways were not predictable from the initial states or initial acts
alone but that 'prediction is *contingent* on the state of affairs
following each move', and hence incorporated assumptions shared
by multi-causal and typological approaches:

> The theory may, of course, contemplate more than one pathway
> to deviance, or different pathways leading to different kinds of
> deviant actions as well as to conformity. Theories constructed on
> the tree model may also be used to explain or predict movement
> from deviance, one or more pathways leading to restoration to
> conformity, others to continued or intensified deviance. The test

of interaction theories is how well observed pathways correspond to those which the theory would predict.
[Cohen, 1966, p. 45]

Cohen's commitment to a single general theory based on prediction rendered his model less radical than it might have been. Other sociologists of deviance have taken the 'processual' or 'sequential' analysis of deviant careers very much further, including the example of Howard Becker's study of becoming a marihuana-user:

> We need a model which takes into account the fact that patterns of behavior *develop* in orderly sequence. In accounting for an individual's use of marihuana ... we must deal with a sequence of steps, of changes in the individual's behavior and perspectives in order to understand the phenomenon. Each step requires explanation, and what may operate as a cause at one step in the sequence may be of negligible importance at another step. . . . The explanation of each step is thus part of the explanation of the resulting behavior. Yet the variables which account for each step may not, taken separately, distinguish between users and non-users.
> [Becker, 1963, p. 23]

Becker contrasted this approach with the traditional 'simultaneous' model, according to which causes were believed to operate at the same time, and the basic objectives were to discover the causes of deviance as social pathology in need of control. Once a theory of the process of marihuana use has been constructed in this step-wise fashion, the kind of explanation that emerges is very different from traditional theories, and provides the basis for a more adequate understanding of the behaviour being studied.

As a further illustration, Matza's image of 'delinquent drift' has many apparent similarities with Cohen's version of interaction; but whereas Cohen seemed to envisage interaction as part and parcel of traditional 'positivist' explanations and prediction of behaviour at the individual level, Matza conceived of his alternative image of 'drift' as a realistic outcome of accepting the implications of 'soft determinism', enabling him to restore a kind of freedom of choice to the individual as a bridge between positivist and classical views of man (Matza, 1964, p. 27). However, in Matza's elaboration of his concept of drift it seems that he has over-reacted to his own version of positivist determinism:

> Drift is motion guided gently by underlying influences. The guidance is gentle and not constraining. The drift may be initiated

or deflected by events so numerous as to defy codification. But underlying influences are operative nonetheless in that they make initiation to delinquency more probable and they reduce the chances that an event will deflect the drifter from his delinquent path. Drift is a gradual process of movement, unperceived by the actor, in which the first stage may be accidental or unpredictable from the point of view of any theoretic frame of reference, and deflection from the delinquent path may be similarly accidental and unpredictable. This does not preclude a general theory of delinquency. However, the major purpose of such a theory is a description of the conditions that make delinquent drift possible and probable, and not a specification of invariant conditions of delinquency.
[Matza, 1964, p. 29]

Despite his self-proclaimed radicalism, Matza failed to restore any meaningful freedom of choice to delinquents in the situation of drift; he still tended to equate theory solely with notions of predictability and probability, and appeared to ignore the possibility of other forms of valid explanation of delinquency, even that which has subjective meaning for the actor. Somewhat trivially, using the same analogy, it would clearly have been possible after the event to explain why certain pieces of driftwood ended up by the river bank, others lodged on rocks in midstream, while yet others were swept over the weir (!) — but Matza neither met nor apparently recognized the challenge implicit in this early conceptualization. (For later development of his ideas see Matza 1969; also Wiles and Beyleveld, 1975.)

Surprisingly, perhaps, we can find in Sutherland's and Cressey's long-established text on *Principles of Criminology* further ideas to support our basic approach. They distinguished two types of explanation: (1) historical or 'genetic', corresponding to the traditional specification of background features in the social structure or the individual, and (2) 'mechanistic-situational', which acknowledged the dynamic role of the situation of crime, both at the objective and subjective levels:

The objective situation is important to criminality largely to the extent that it provides an opportunity for a criminal act. . . . The situation is not exclusive of the person, for the situation which is important is the situation as defined by the person who is involved. . . . The events in the person-situation complex at the time of crime occurs cannot be separated from the prior life experiences of the criminal.
[Sutherland and Cressey, 1970, pp. 74-5]

Accepting a framework of this kind would entail an analysis of the 'objective' crime situation, investigation of the background factors in the individual or social group, and close attention to the subjective meaning attached to the situation by the actor. The possible outcome of such an integrated approach could be an extremely satisfying explanation of specific criminal acts, although the very complexity of the task should warn against expecting any significant generalizations to emerge beyond the results of the particular crime 'inquest'.

In Cressey's own study of embezzlement, *Other People's Money* (1971), we have what can be seen as an applied and extended version of the same idea. Cressey's explicit theoretical objectives here were somewhat indirectly linked to the concept of 'analytic induction' (see Znaniecki, 1934; Robinson, 1951), and he conceived the exercise as an ambitious attempt at 'social-scientific explanation'. He was careful to define his subject-matter in non-legal terms as 'criminal trust violation', and set himself the task of 'determining whether a definable sequence or conjuncture of events is always present when criminal trust violation is present and never present when trust violation is absent' (Cressey, 1971, p. 12). He recognized the importance of situational factors and how a person's background would influence his interpretation of the situation in which he found himself:

> A specific type of reaction in a specific situation might be necessary for trust violation and if such a reaction is present trust violation may be explained in terms of it. However, the reaction itself must be explained in terms of the life experience of the person.
> [Cressey, 1971, p. 13]

As the research progressed it became obvious to Cressey that the origin of trust violation could not be attributed to any single event or 'cause', but that 'its explanation could be made only in terms of a series or conjuncture of events, a process' (Cressey, 1971, p. 29). What we have here is a useful example of a narrative explanation (or a grouped series of such explanations) of embezzling activity, which would have had tremendous merit on those terms alone without the methodological and theoretical deep water in which Cressey placed himself in elaborating a more complex theory of criminal trust violation, aiming as near as possible to universal generalizations built up by the process of analytic induction. Once these theoretical claims were made, it was relatively easy for critics to show that his methodology was inadequate to the task he had set himself. Ironically, many of these very same criticisms strengthened the claim of work of this kind as retrospective explanations. In this rather different light, the 'universal generalizations' attacked by Turner (1953) as mere *definitions* could be extremely useful as defining classes of criminal behaviour that share certain situational elements or subjective interpretations, and could well constitute the groundwork for constructing preliminary typologies of crime. Finally, like any explanation that derives its power from its 'adequacy at the level of meaning', the methods of analytic induction may often be able to provide meaningful explanations for statistical correlations (see Turner, 1953).

It was on the basis of the framework of ideas suggested by Sutherland and Cressey that Don Gibbons advocated the shifting of criminological attention 'away from person-oriented perspectives toward more concern with criminogenic situations' (Gibbons, 1971, p. 268). He claimed that crime often 'grew out of events closely tied to the location and time of the deviant act' which could not be predicted on the basis of 'historical' or 'genetic' information alone:

> In many cases, criminality may be a response to nothing more temporal than the provocations and attractions bound up in the immediate circumstances. It may be that, in some kinds of lawbreaking, understanding of that behaviour may require detailed attention to the concatenation of events immediately preceding it.
> [Gibbons, 1971, p. 272]

Gibbons did not envisage the criminological task as involving an exclusive choice between 'historical-genetic' or 'mechanistic-situational-dynamic' processes for explaining crime, but rather that of analysing each instance according to the relative contribution of its past and present situational elements. Providing that the emphasis upon situational factors did not in turn become too exaggerated and single-minded, but was considered along with background characteristics and an assessment of subjective meaning, such a change of direction would be beneficial for criminology. It accords with the identified need for statistics of crime to become more consumer-oriented and to include more focus upon the crime event; it could provide the basis for the classification of certain groups of crime, independent of a typology of offenders; and, most importantly, it would recognize the essentially unpredictable nature of so much crime and delinquency, in which given the right combination of circumstances and motivation any one of us might become involved, even if not detected!

CHAPTER 3

Criminal Justice

Organizational goals and discipline impose a set of demands and conditions of practice on respective professions in the criminal court, to which they respond by abandoning their ideological and professional commitments to the accused client, in the service of these higher claims of the court organization. [Blumberg, 1967, p. 49]

Openness is the natural enemy of arbitrariness and a natural ally in the fight against injustice. [Davis, 1969, p. 98]

A feature that is absent from all but the most recent period in the development of criminology is serious attention being paid to those stages in the 'criminalization' process which intervene between legislation and the application of penal measures to convicted offenders. 'Crime' and 'punishment' have been given their due in the past but the intervening processes of criminal justice have been relatively ignored. The present generation of criminologists are more than making up for the omissions of their predecessors, and criminal justice research is now asserting itself in some countries to such an extent that it is in danger of distorting the balance within criminology. For these reasons it is essential to examine some of the relevant developments in this aspect of the subject, showing once again the handicaps imposed by the positivist framework of its past history, and emphasizing the centrality of value judgements in any critique of the processes of criminal justice.

IMAGES OF THE LAW IN ACTION

In the relatively short history of the systematic study of law enforcement and the administration of criminal justice, undoubtedly the most common approach adopted by researchers has been that of a positivist empiricism focused on the discovery of disparities between decision-makers at various stages of the process from police arrest to the verdicts and sentences of the criminal courts. Particularly in the early days of research into sentencing disparities between different judges, the value of such studies was mainly at the level of descriptive *revelations* of the apparent inequities in the system, rather than in terms of theoretical *explanations* of decision-making. The approach was selective and piecemeal, showing little awareness of the importance of the relationships between different groups of decision-makers. 'Justice' was equated with 'uniformity', with little critical attention paid to the question of overall objectives or criteria against which uniformity could be assessed. In other words, the concept of justice associated with this sort of research tended to be of a limited procedural or comparative kind, based on an assumption that a consensus existed on desirable objectives in criminal justice. These admittedly rather overdrawn characteristics of the dominant 'liberal reform' approach to the analysis of criminal justice illustrate some of the main dimensions of our examination of the different images to be found within criminological research into the law in action: research methods vary from positivist empiricism, through participant observation and interactionist analysis, to ethnomethodological accounts; the focus of study ranges from the individual decision-maker operating on his own or in a group, through relationships between decision-makers, to the analysis of criminal justice as a bureaucratic organization; and the objectives of researchers range from the description of disparities to the explanation of basic injustices, often with fundamentally different working assumptions about the meaning of 'justice' in dealing with those suspected of criminal offences. For purposes of discussion we shall distinguish between three broad approaches, according to the focus of attention: (1) *disparities among decision-makers,* (2) *divergent working philosophies* in law enforcement and criminal justice agencies, and (3) *bureaucracy and bargaining.* Although I shall attempt to illustrate the typical differences between these approaches, along the lines of the dimensions already indicated, this classification is not intended as a constraining framework into which all research must be fitted. It is simply put forward as a useful way of organizing the discussion that will hopefully further our understanding of past trends and clarify future options.

Disparities among decision-makers: liberal pragmatism

My study of *Decisions in the Penal Process* (Bottomley, 1973), documented relevant research findings for a selection of the decision-stages in criminal justice, and showed the pervasiveness of the concern to describe and explain disparities. The earliest research of this kind was carried out in America during the first decades of this century, focusing upon sentencing patterns of individual judges, and it is significant that the 'explanations' offered were usually in terms of the 'human element' involved in such decisions, reflecting the individuality of judges and the 'personal equation' in sentencing. A survey of the findings of sentencing research of the last fifty years suggested that the most persuasive evidence seemed to support a similar view that 'the most fundamental influences upon sentencing behaviour are the penal philosophies and attitudes of individual magistrates' (Bottomley, 1973, p. 169). Although I would no longer wish to subscribe to such a simplistic interpretation of the available data, the fact is that this 'human factor' theme recurs throughout research within this tradition with a persistence comparable to that of individual theories of criminal behaviour. It is perhaps similarly explicable as due at least in part to society's unwillingness to entertain explanations with more serious implications, for more far-reaching reform in the organization of criminal justice and the structure of society.

Apart from attempts to explain disparities in terms of the individual characteristics of the decision-makers, some important studies have emphasized the need to widen the scope of investigation to incorporate the possible influence of community characteristics. Roger Hood's (1962) study of the use of prison sentences for property offenders revealed that the magistrates in more middle-class and 'community-conscious' towns tended to be more severe in their sentencing practice than did those in towns of a greater social mix.

In the field of police studies, J.Q. Wilson's (1968) analysis of different styles of policing in eight American communities showed that there was often a close relationship between the social composition of an area and the exercise of police discretion in peace-keeping and law enforcement. Similarly, in her research in an English county police force, Maureen Cain (1973) illustrated how rural police work seemed to be directly influenced by the definitions of what was important by the people of the local community.

The potential explanatory power of studies such as these which consider aspects of the local environment in which the law is being administered is considerably greater than those which are more narrowly focused upon the personal characteristics of decision-makers, but one of their common weaknesses is the absence of any theoretical perspective that would allow judgements to be made either as to the appropriateness of community influence upon criminal justice or about desirable criteria for the administration of justice. To describe disparities and identify bias is a necessary step towards the elimination of injustice but in itself can resolve nothing, unless there is an agreed yardstick against which what is discovered can be measured. Pepinsky was right to draw attention to the relationship between knowledge and justice, in his provocative essay on criminal justice in the contemporary American context:

> The *appearance* of just applications of the law can only be maintained in the absence of knowledge of what the biases may be. Inversely, studies in which biases are inferred serve merely to indicate the doing of injustice; they cannot facilitate maintenance of the appearance of doing justice. In the final analysis, information as to sources of . . . bias can be used to select biases, but in this form of social engineering injustice will appear where once it was assumed that justice was being done.
> [Pepinsky, 1976, pp. 52-3]

Pepinsky believed that 'justice' could only be done as long as the (inevitable) biases of decision-makers remained unknown, but that once these biases were systematically documented then all possibility of 'justice' disappeared. However, instead of attempting to justify a concept of justice based on *unknown biases,* it seems to me that it would be more desirable to pursue the quest for *open justice* based on as full a knowledge as possible of existing biases, which could then be subjected to proper public evaluation, as the basis for policy and practice.

As far as concerns us at this stage, it is merely necessary to be aware of the characteristic fashion in which much research into disparities failed to ask crucial questions about criteria of criminal justice, and usually failed to present an argued case for the preference of certain biases over others. This absence of critical awareness of the wider questions that needed asking was undoubtedly partly due to an assumption of a broadly-based consensus about objectives to be found within the community of 'liberal reformers', as suggested by Colin Low's recently published review of trends in the sociology of criminal justice in Britain:

> As far as research is concerned, therefore, rational liberal values have prevailed. . . . Liberalism has ensured that research in the criminal justice area has assumed a social administration rather than a strictly sociological character, at least as far as this country is concerned. . . . The officially stated goals of the system are largely taken for granted, and the sole concern is with the means by which they are realised. This leads to the research having a pragmatic quality. The accent everywhere is empirical.
> [Low, 1978, p. 15]

Certainly in the context of academic criminology, wherever disparities have been revealed it has been too often and too easily assumed that the direction in which change (towards 'uniformity') should occur was obvious. As a consequence of this failure to be more explicit about underlying values, the possibility of meaningful dialogue between researchers and practitioners has been seriously impeded, and in terms of progress towards a critical analysis of criminal justice, basic first principles tend to have been ignored in favour of second-order concepts of procedural and comparative justice. Within the dominant liberal-pragmatic approach there has been increasing support for the introduction of due process measures to guarantee the reality of legal rights for suspects, from the time when they are first interviewed by the police through to the process of trial and sentence. Whatever the actual reasons may be for apparent disparities in the application of the law, it is widely believed that some of the grosser inequalities can be removed by ensuring that common procedures are followed and that all suspects are offered genuine opportunities to exercise their rights. We shall be examining later the contribution that due process measures can make to a fully-fledged concept of justice, but it is important to note here that this contribution can only properly be assessed in relationship to agreed overall objectives of the criminal justice process, which is precisely what the empirical positivists generally failed to tackle in any explicit or effective way.

To be fair to the traditional approach to the explanation of disparities, recent years have seen some developments that are far removed from the earlier lack of sophistication and somewhat complacent satisfaction with explanations of the individualistic kind. In parallel with the legalistic emphasis upon the need for greater due process at all stages, there has developed an awareness among some criminologists of the importance of structural and 'operational' aspects of decision-making. At the simplest level, this has been reflected in the officially recognized need for the provision of relevant information to aid the task of decision-makers. In Britain the best example of this kind has been the increasing use of social enquiry reports before sentence, following the recommendations of the Streatfeild Committee (Home Office, 1961; also see Davies, 1974). A rather less spectacular example has been Home Office encouragement for the systematic provision of information upon persons applying for pre-trial bail. Nevertheless, even these developments have proceeded in something of a critical vacuum, as if the mere provision of information would automatically improve decision-making or clarify objectives (see Bottomley, 1977).

Moving to a rather different kind of analysis, there have been applications of 'decision-games' theory to criminal justice, along the lines pioneered by Leslie Wilkins, and used for the analysis of decisions by magistrates, probations officers and police (Wilkins, 1964; Wilkins and Chandler, 1965; Sullivan and Siegel, 1972). Despite the artificiality and somewhat contrived nature of some of this work, it can make a valuable contribution towards an understanding of the relationship between information and objectives, and illustrates the different strategies adopted for handling information and reaching decisions.

Finally, reference must be made to the ambitious attempt by Hood and Sparks (1970, pp. 156-70) to construct a model of the structure of the sentencing process, as a framework for analysing one of the central decision-stages in criminal justice. This model identified the major elements in the sentencing decision, and allowed for the incorporation of relevant data beyond the narrow confines of traditional empiricism. It focused attention upon the complex linkages between the judge, the aims of penal measures, information about the offence and the offender, and the choice of sentence. The role of legal rules and conventions was taken into account, as was the part played by those who provide information for the courts, such as police, lawyers and the probation service. The judge was analysed not only according to traditional personal variables but also according to 'role variables' relating to his office as a judge; and the way in which he categorized available information on the offence and offender was related to his views on the aims of sentencing. In a subsequent study of the sentencing of motoring offenders, Hood (1972) came to the conclusion that a major explanation of disparities in these cases was to be found in 'the way in which magistrates learn their sentencing trade and local benches develop their policies', thereby confirming the emphasis placed earlier upon the influence of 'judicial role variables'. However, even if it were possible to acquire sufficient knowledge to validate a complex model like this, the basic limitation of the exercise still remains. It was inherent in Hood and Sparks' conception of criminology's role in the study of criminal justice and penal policy, according to which it can provide 'disinterested and purely scientific research' on the operation of the processes, but 'what it cannot do is decide what the *aims* of penal policy should be' (Hood and Sparks, 1970, p. 9). We believe that such a restricting view of criminology is no longer tenable, but that the issues of the aims and values of criminal justice and penal theory must be treated as absolutely central.

Divergent working philosophies: the displacement of justice

The focus of traditional criminal justice research upon individual disparities reflected an uncritical assumption of consensus within society about penal objectives, and resulted in a corresponding lack of awareness of possible dissensus within and between the various agencies involved in the processing of 'offenders'. The typical research strategy entailed a concentration upon specific categories of decision-makers, considered in relative isolation from the rest, and the reliance upon a narrow range of empirical methods tended not to reveal those aspects of the situation that might have disturbed the dominant conceptions. Such compartmentalization in the analysis of criminal justice gave rise to little apprehension about distorting what was being studied, because it was tacitly assumed that common objectives characterized the entire process. We can see, therefore, that a central paradox of traditional research was the coexistence of a belief in the essential unity of purpose within the system, together with a practical strategy characterized by its piecemeal treatment of decision-stages in isolation from one another, which in turn could only but leave unchallenged the tenability of the overall view.

Significant changes of perspective and method were heralded by detailed participant observation studies of police behaviour in the United States during the 1950s and 1960s (see, for example, Westley, 1953, 1970; Skolnick, 1966; Bordua, 1967; Niederhoffer, 1969). These sociological studies illustrated how the main constraint upon the way police exercised their wide discretion derived from the 'working philosophies' that had emerged to cope with the personal and organizational demands of the job. They provided the paradigm for what seems an essential first step towards understanding the operation of the law in action. The notion of 'people doing a job', according to their personal or professional lights, illuminates not only police practices but those of other key groups intervening between arrest and sentence, including prosecutors, lawyers and social workers. A crucial characteristic to which attention was drawn early in the study of the exercise of police discretion (see Goldstein, 1960) is that of the 'low-visibility' of many of the occasions when suspects and defendants are involved with police, lawyers and other official personnel. This makes it very difficult for any 'outsider' to know for certain what takes place in the privacy of a police station, a solicitor's office or jury room. The likelihood of informal and private justice being administered in such situations is increased by the extreme vulnerability of the suspect's position.

The main handicap to the attainment of integrated criminal justice is not, however, the inherent 'low-visibility' of so much that goes on but the *diversification of objectives* among the different groups involved, so that justice is displaced by short-term goals that are perceived as more appropriate for practical purposes. This 'displacement of justice' in favour of more attainable objectives is not simply the fault of the occupational groups directly involved but stems directly from society's own ambiguity and failure to articulate any clear policy for criminal justice. A.J. Reiss has spelled out the consequences:

Each organization creates its own system of justice, a system of

justice without trial. The police . . . do justice by illegal arrest, improper use of force and harassment. The prosecutor institution-alizes falsification by the 'justice' of plea bargaining. Defendants are told to plead to matters that state falsely the nature of their violation of the law. The defendant, defence counsel, and the prosecutor deny in response to a necessary query from the judge that there has been a prior bargain, and the judge accepts the plea of guilty with full awareness that a bargain that has been denied has been struck.
[Reiss, 1974, p. 73; emphasis added]

Implicit in this perspective, therefore, is the denial of any possibility of adequate justice to the hapless defendant (except on a purely random basis), who is passed from one stage of the process to the next regardless of the lack of integration either in working relationships or guiding principles.

The police provide the most well documented case-study for illustrating something of the origins and consequences of the influence of 'working philosophies' in the different subsystems of law enforcement and criminal justice. An important contributory element has been the way in which the police have looked (in part) to the community being policed for definitions of their role. This was stressed by Westley (1953, 1970) in one of the earliest studies of police in America, and was placed in a broader context by Michael Banton:

The police are given a variety of objectives but they are simultaneously subjected to a host of restrictions concerning the ways in which they may attain them, and the interplay between ends and means is much more complex than in most organizations. The efficiency of the police may therefore be less important than their responsiveness to the community they are required to serve.
[Banton, 1964, pp. 105-6]

Banton's final sentence could almost be rephrased to suggest that in fact the efficiency of the police is often *defined* by the extent to which they respond appropriately to the concerns of the community. Westley went so far as to 'justify' police use of violence as carrying out the implicit mandate of the community to solve serious crime; but he was not so naive as to be unaware of the way in which the 'resource of violence' could be appropriated by the police to serve more purely personal ends in establishing respect for their status and authority, with the result that occupational legitimation could in time come to supercede that derived from the law:

Their general legitimation of the use of violence *primarily* in terms of coercing respect and making a 'good pinch' clearly points out the existence of occupational goals, which are independent of and take precedence over the legal mandate. The existence of such goals and patterns of conduct indicates that the policeman has made of his occupation a preoccupation and invested in it a large aspect of his self.
[Westley, 1953, p. 41]

Subsequent studies by Wilson (1968) in America and Cain (1973) in England confirmed how in certain circumstances the police interpret their role and exercise their discretion in direct response to community definitions. Wilson's 'service style' of policing existed in middle-class communities, in which the police were directly exposed to community concerns for public order and consequently took seriously problems and requests for police intervention. Similarly, in her comparison between rural and city definitions of police work in England, Maureen Cain showed how 'real' police work meant different things in the two forces because of the differences in community expectations. The city police, who worked in a heterogeneous community in which the only identifiable consensus on the police role was centred on the narrow area of crime control, fell back on crime work as their primary defining task. When not much crime work came their way the city beat men would often make do with lesser 'prisoner-getting' activity such as arresting drunks; but they would also search out 'action' and indulge in 'easing' behaviour by way of a compensation for the lack of 'real police work' (Cain, 1973, pp. 69ff.). By contrast, the rural one-man beat men worked in communities with a much greater degree of consensus about police work:

The crimes may have been defined as 'petty' by city men, but they were defined as important by the rural men who had to deal with them. *The people of the community defined them as important, and had power to define them for their policeman.* Because the community defined them as important, dealing with these crimes had the legitimating effect from which I have argued the high status of crime work is derived. Moreover, the rural man did not define his task purely in terms of crime.
[Cain, 1973, p. 71]

Unfortunately, the problems of contemporary policing are firmly located in the urban environment of our big cities where neither community nor consensus on 'law and order' are readily identifiable. The police are thus increasingly pushed back onto their own internal resources and assessments of aims and efficiency. At the same time there are internal pressures from police management towards greater 'professionalism', so that the officer on the beat has the unenviable task of interpreting the mandate of law and order for himself with little guidance from the community he is policing, while attempting to reconcile this with the operational requirements of emergent police professionalism.

Jerome Skolnick highlighted these dilemmas in his seminal work on police behaviour, *Justice Without Trial: Law Enforcement in Democratic Society*. He interpreted the phrase 'law and order' in the police context, primarily as a requirement that they *maintain order under the rule of law*; but he saw this as creating tension between 'the operational consequences of ideas of order, efficiency and initiative on the one hand, and legality, on the other', particularly in guaranteeing the rights of individual citizens:

> The procedures of the criminal law, therefore, stress protection of individual liberties *within* a system of social order. This dichotomy suggests that the common juxtaposition of 'law and order' is an oversimplification. Law is not merely an instrument of order but may frequently be its adversary.
> [Skolnick, 1966, p. 7]

Skolnick was using 'law' here in two different senses: he had already shown that the police frequently use the law as an *instrument of order,* in the sense that substantive legislation provided them with grounds for arrest or other coercive action; but, on the other hand, the *due procedures* required by law are often viewed by the police as hinderances to the successful carrying out of their crime control and order maintenance mandates. It was also suggested by Skolnick that the occupational culture of the police undermined the idea that the rule of law was the primary objective of police work, either in the sense of law enforcement, as a major end in itself, or of due procedures of law as an essential means of police work. The combined effects of the police working personality, socialization into the job, and the opportunities provided by the low-visibility of police-citizen encounters, resulted in 'goal displacement' in response to the need to maintain personal authority in the handling of situations and in response to the pressure to be productive in terms of efficient (rather than strictly legal) crime work (Skolnick, 1966,

p. 231). The policeman was portrayed as a *craftsman* rather than a '*legal* actor'; as such, 'the policeman views criminal procedure with the administrative bias of the craftsman, a prejudice contradictory to due process of law' (Skolnick, 1966, p. 19), and he tends to resent those critics who measure his value against abstract principles of legality and criminal justice rather than against the reality of his workaday world.

The decline of meaningful communities from which police might in theory derive definitions of their role, combined in recent years with pressures within police management towards increased professionalism, seems to have strengthened the influence of the occupational culture as the prime definer of the police task. Former American police officer, Arthur Niederhoffer, graphically portrayed the philosophy of 'cynicism' which he claimed had quickly come to dominate the police subculture, in response to a pervasive sense of anomie, involving 'loss of faith in people, of enthusiasm for the high ideals of police work, and of pride and integrity' (Niederhoffer, 1969, p. 96). He described the 'reality shock' of the new police recruit:

> The rookie begins with faith in the system. He tries to follow the book of rules and regulations. . . . He is chastised by his colleagues for being naive enough to follow the book. Gradually he learns to neglect the formal rules and norms and turns elsewhere for direction. Individual interpretation replaces the formal authoritative dictum of the official book and the young policeman is an easy prey to cynicism.
> [Niederhoffer, 1969, pp. 52-3]

In an early paper, James Q. Wilson (1963) suggested that the typical police response to the problem of morale involved the two different codes of (1) 'the system', and (2) professionalism. The 'system' was 'the institutionalized rules and norms which express the policeman's position as a member of a group which feels keenly its pariah status'; by professionalism Wilson meant 'an institutionalization of rules and norms expressing not feelings of group separateness, but an external body of "expert" knowledge about "correct" police work'. Neither code however is an entirely satisfactory way of meeting the need for solidarity; the system can be divisive as well as integrating, in its denial of certain official rules and implicit encouragement of suspicion within the ranks. Furthermore, both codes are ways of keeping the community at a distance and occasionally denying its authority altogether.

In his subsequent study of varieties of police behaviour, Wilson elaborated upon Skolnick's concept of the policeman as craftsman, particularly in so far as police work could only be learned by *'apprenticeship'*, and emphasized that craft membership signalled a rejection of images of the policeman either as bureaucrat or as professional — 'an attempt to change a craft into a bureaucracy will be perceived by the members as a failure of confidence and a withdrawal of support and thus strongly resisted; efforts to change it into a profession will be seen as irrelevant and thus largely ignored' (Wilson, 1968, p. 283).

Simon Holdaway (1977) has provided evidence of similar constraints and tensions within urban policing in England, again writing with the inside knowledge of an ex-police officer, and supplementing the data of Maureen Cain whose research was carried out before the emphasis upon professionalization developed in the British police service during the late 1960s and 1970s. Among the main principles of 'managerial professionalism' that Holdaway identified were (1) 'informed discretion', and the desirability of working within the legal rules governing the collection of evidence; (2) increased accountability, and the establishment of a 'consensus of consent'; and (3) broader based assessment of police work, beyond the narrow 'crime and arrest' orientation typically found among urban police. It seems very clear from his detailed accounts that the actual definitions of police work that influence urban policemen are far removed from the official expectations of 'managerial professionalism'. The searching out of action and excitement are still very much the dominant features of everyday police work, together with a preoccupation with the economics and significance of arrests and charge statistics (Holdaway, 1977, pp. 126-31; see also Walsh, 1977). The continuing dominance of the values and control strategies of the occupational culture of the lower ranks within the police force reflect the 'practical professionalism' that we have already seen highlighted by the American descriptions of the police as craftsmen:

> Practical professionalism remains a series of hedonistic, protective and highly practical activities and values which are largely opposed to those of managerial professionalism. Practical professionalism represents the routine policing of urban Britain.
> [Holdaway, 1977, p. 134]

Practical professionalism is more than just a matter of learning when *not* to go by the book, and involves a far-reaching reorientation towards traditional definitions of the police function and its relationship to law and justice.

It is now an accepted element of conventional wisdom in police studies to assert the important distinction between 'law enforcement' and 'peace-keeping' or 'order-maintenance', as well as to stress the 'public service' or 'support' role of the police, which in time and effort constitutes a growing part of police work (see Cumming *et al.*, 1965; Bottomley, 1973, ch. 2). However, the role of law in police work is more subtle and complicated than implied in some of the discussions. In the first place, the practical constraints of the face-to-face situations that confront police officers often means that a vital initial concern is that of establishing that degree of personal authority which is an essential precondition of effective action of any kind. This strongly-felt need for 'respect' explains many facets of the behaviour and working philosophy of the police, from the importance attached to 'demeanor' and 'cooperation' of those being questioned to the occupational justification of violence (see Piliavin and Briar, 1964; Westley, 1970; Reiss, 1971).

For a number of reasons, the mandate of 'enforcing the law' is particularly unhelpful. The need for the exercise of discretion and selective enforcement is widely accepted by the occupational subculture, and to a lesser extent at the official managerial levels. The result is that in a very real sense the police are 'practical legislators':

> It is the individual policeman's responsibility to decide if and how the law should be applied, and he searches for the proper combination of cues on which to base his decision. Because the application of the law depends to a large degree on the patrolman, he, in effect, makes the law; it is his decision that establishes the boundary between legal and illegal.
> [Niederhoffer, 1969, p. 64]

The influence of what Wilson (1963) called the code of the 'system' is often paramount in determining the ultimate shape of that police-made law. In other words, it would appear that the law is rarely enforced for its own sake; it can be, as Skolnick suggested, primarily used as an instrument for the maintenance of order, but it can also serve essential purposes in terms of the maintenance of occupational solidarity. In his closely observed studies of police handling of drunks on skid-row and the exercise of discretion in the compulsory detention of the mentally ill, Egon Bittner (1967a, 1967b) illustrated how the police frequently used the law and their powers of arrest in order to achieve their objectives as 'peace officers'. He concluded that 'in real police work *the provisions contained in the law represent a resource that can be invoked* to handle certain problems', and that particularly in discretionary situations where invoking the law is not a foregone conclusion 'it is only speciously true to say that the law determined the act of apprehension, and much more correct to say that the law made the action possible' (Bittner, 1967a, p. 278).

The research of Michael Chatterton in England has confirmed that this conceptualization is equally valid for understanding police behaviour in this country, with legal arrest powers perceived as 'resources to be used to achieve the ends of those who are entitled or able to use them' (Chatterton, 1976, p. 114). Chatterton showed how in the use of certain public order charges, especially drunk and disorderly, and others such as assaults against the person, there were often very different reasons behind the decisions to use a charge as 'the legal vehicle for conveying someone to the police station' from the *post hoc* justification provided to the courts; in particular, the police were concerned to avoid 'trouble', both 'within-the-job' from their supervising officers and 'on-the-job' in continuing relationships with the community being policed. In the context of 'on-the-job' trouble the police were very sensitive to any incident that might appear to threaten their control over a specific geo-graphical area for which they were responsible, but would only use their powers of arrest as a last resort (Chatterton, 1976, p. 118).

However much the values of 'practical professionalism' within the police appear to be opposed to the idea of law enforcement for its own sake, and stress the role of the police as 'craftsmen' rather than 'legal actors', in reality they are legal actors *par excellence,* dispensing a justice which is often informal and because of its low-visibility essentially *unaccountable* either to internal or external assessment. The working philosophy of the police is centrally concerned with the administration of a form of justice, but it is not often the justice of the courtrooms. It has even been argued that it expresses a 'higher' ideal than the law itself — namely, 'to deal with the problems with which the law itself is intended to deal' (Goldstein, 1977, p. 34). Many police decisions have to be taken quickly in the thick of a practical situation, so that ready-made prejudgements (prejudices?) inevitably come into play, centred round police concerns with 'blame' and assessment of 'moral character'. It is not only at the more formal stages of decisions about the nature of official proceedings against suspects that there is a conflict as to the respective roles of the police and the judiciary. Chatterton illustrated differences of opinion at the earlier stages of police intervention, with some officers believing that it was 'unprofessional' to consider issues of 'blame' in determining the use of arrest powers:

> [They felt that] . . . if an offence had been committed and there was a prima facie case against an identified suspect the police officer's role was to take the necessary steps to detain him and bring him before the court. To take on the function of judge and jury by trying to decide who was to blame, was to be swayed by sentiment and to assume a prerogative to which police officers were not entitled.
> [Chatterton, 1976, p. 119]

It seems clear, therefore, that police decisions to arrest a suspect or achieve their objectives by alternative methods are in a very real sense 'judicial', and in many situations the police officer can properly be seen as a dispenser of 'justice without trial'.

Space does not permit us to continue this analysis in detail past the arrest stage, but all the indications suggest that once an arrest has been made (with or without 'good cause') the 'presumption of guilt' pervades much police behaviour in the processes of interrogation, charging and preparing the case for trial. For the police to work without such a presumption would tend to undermine the justification, in their own minds, for the earlier decision to arrest. Regarded in this light, the nature of police involvement in the pre-trial process becomes more understandable. In the questioning of suspects, the discovery of material evidence, police attitudes towards the official rights of suspects for legal assistance and their opposition to the granting of bail, 'crime control' values reign supreme (see Packer, 1969, ch. 8). To the extent that the police are seen by those they arrest or suspect of crime as 'doing their job', that job is the control of crime by ensuring the conviction of those they have already so often prejudged to be guilty.

The last word on the police can appropriately be left to the consumers of justice. In Casper's survey of defendants' perspectives upon criminal justice in America, he identified a strong sense of 'resignation' in suspects once they had been arrested; for most of them their case was virtually over by this stage, and what happened between then and the court's sentence was simply a matter of machinations over the specific form of sentence (Casper, 1972, p. 34). This view of arrest as the end of the matter rather than its mere beginning, in legal terms, is uncannily similar to the police view of the situation. Casper's sample of defendants saw the police as mainly involved in the business of 'criminal catching':

> Because it is a job, it is likened to other occupations in our economic system: there is a production ethic, good work (many arrests) is rewarded, and each man is generally attempting to better himself in his organization. Occasionally you encounter a rate buster — an overzealous officer who tries too hard — but most police officers are simply workers in an organization.
> [Casper, 1972, p. 38]

The theme that runs throughout Casper's book is that the defendant's experience of the criminal justice process is entirely comparable to his experience of upbringing and 'street-life' in which 'nobody is neutral or detached or impartial — everyone has his job and he does it'; people are treated as objects or adversaries rather than individuals, and justice is sacrificed on the altar of the production ethic (Casper, 1972, p. 50).

The police are not the only group of 'professionals' involved in the low-visibility stages of criminal justice, but the wealth of comparative information available on their day-to-day work makes them a prime example of the theme of divergent working philosophies in criminal justice. Provided that equally thorough evidence is forthcoming, a similar approach seems likely to illuminate other versions of 'private justice' dispensed out of court by prosecutors, lawyers and social workers. As the picture is gradually built up from research into these other professional groups it will become increasingly important to discover the source of the different working philosophies and the factors that contribute to their maintenance in the occupational cultures. The outlines of this picture so far suggest that a crucial element is provided by the conception of the criminal justice process as a bureaucracy, primarily concerned with bargaining and negotiated justice, to which we must now turn our attention.

Bureaucracy and bargaining: routine justice and the production ethic

The two approaches to the study of criminal justice that have been identified so far were both inclined (although for different reasons) to ignore the issue of relationships within the system and interconnections between the decision-stages. Empirical positivists generally took for granted that all parts of the system were working relatively harmoniously towards the same official goals, whereas the sociologists of occupational cultures within criminal justice assumed that for all practical purposes each group was only concerned with its own strictly limited goals and production targets, paying little regard to the wider context or consequences of their decisions. However, there were signs within both these traditions of the need to question the consensual image of the criminal justice process, to recognize the different ways in which decisions taken at one stage were influenced by and had an impact upon those at other stages, and to analyse more closely the negotiated reality of the relationships within the bureaucratic organization of the administration of justice. Thus, the image of a production-conscious bureaucracy and of a bargain justice of the market-place came to be favoured by criminologists attempting to comprehend the social reality of the law in action.

Evidence began to emerge from conventional studies, focused on disparities at a single stage of the criminal justice process, that the scope and nature of the exercise of discretion by a particular group of decision-makers were crucially affected by decisions taken earlier in the process: sentencing was influenced by the extent to which the police siphoned off minor offenders in various ways; the granting of pre-trial bail by the courts was affected by local policy in the use of police bail; and, in its turn, a remand in custody appeared to have some influence upon the subsequent choice of plea by a defendant or even the finding of guilt and type of sentence imposed. It also became clear that the different official parties involved at any particular stage (not to mention the defendant whose viewpoint was not usually taken into account) often perceived the same situation from different perspectives, so that the final outcome was either an unprincipled compromise or a victory by one side or another that merely accentuated the extent of disparity or sense of injustice. Bail decisions commonly provided the setting for the presentation of diverse views on the role of pre-trial custody, covering the whole gamut from the crime-control attitudes of the police, when opposing bail, to the due process ('presumption of innocence') arguments put forward by the accused's lawyer. Similarly, the sentencing process has come increasingly to involve the probation and social work services in the provision of social enquiry reports, in which the expressed advice and underlying ideologies may not be totally compatible with the judicial frame of reference.

Preliminary indications, suggesting the interconnectedness of the criminal justice process, received authoritative confirmation from the major programme of research launched by the American Bar Foundation in the 1950s. Although this research was broadly within the category of 'liberal pragmatism', with each of its impressive research reports focused on a single area of decision-making (LaFave, 1965; Newman, 1966; Tiffany *et al.*, 1967; Miller, 1969; Dawson, 1969), the organizing framework was there for a potentially more radical appreciation of the processes at work. Donald J. Newman subsequently elaborated upon this approach in his 'functional analysis' of criminal justice, based on a 'decision-flow' model, and focused upon the interaction of policies and practices among the various agencies involved:

> The decision-making, functional approach has the advantage of cutting through the provincialism that has characterized criminal justice planning and programing. . . . Decisions made by the police, such as whether or not to invoke the criminal process, and if so, how and how vigorously, are not merely in-house concerns. What the police do, or do not do, has a pervasive effect across the system, as do decisions made in other agencies and offices. This whole approach demonstrates that the criminal justice system is a system not because of bureaucratic structure, for the agencies of crime control are relatively independent, but rather because of the functional relationships among the enforcement efforts of the police, the prosecutory decisions of states' attorneys, the adjudicatory and sentencing functions of trial judges, and the post-conviction treatment of offenders in correctional agencies.
> [Newman, 1975, pp. 6-7]

From the sociological tradition of analysing the working philosophies of occupational groups in law enforcement and the administration of justice came supporting evidence that despite the essentially self-contained values and objectives of each 'subsystem' there was an important sense in which an awareness of the wider system (in relation to which their decisions were both 'input' and 'output') impinged upon practical decision-making. Police studies were once again the main source of an appreciation of this element in relationships with other agencies. We have seen how part of the explanation of the strength of the occupational culture in defining the role of practical policing lay in the need for specified and attainable objectives in police work; although the code of the 'system' set up its own criteria for measuring police efficiency, there was still an apparent hankering after the external confirmation of success that comes with a court conviction and the passing of an appropriate sentence:

> The policeman's triumph comes when the court vindicates his judgement by a conviction. . . . At any rate, a conviction reassures him of his own competence and at the same time of the worth of his job.
> [Westley, 1970, p. 81]

Too often, however, police lack of confidence in the ability or willingness of the courts to support their action results in their settling things outside the courts to ensure that 'justice is done' (Reiss and Bordua, 1967). As a result of police alienation from the justice dispensed by the courts there grows an increasing allegiance to subcultural justice:

> The judgements of the police and of others in the legal system are intricately balanced in a commitment to justice. If, on the average, the officer's sense of justice is not confirmed, or if his moral commitments are not sustained by others, he loses his own moral commitment to the system. Where moral commitment is lost, subcultural practices take over.
> [Reiss, 1971, p. 138]

An extension of this outline of the relationship between the police and judicial authorities to the other sets of relationships within the network of criminal justice agencies confirms Reiss' picture of 'a loosely articulated set of subsystems' characterized more by endemic conflict and disjuncture in values and behaviour than by any sense of common objectives (Reiss and Black, 1967; Reiss, 1971, 1974).

When the focus of attention switched from the police to the other legal actors whose work centred around the business of the criminal courts, it seemed natural to view the operation of the legal system as a bureaucratic organization involved in the business of purveying bargain justice, and committed to the production ethic. Adequate articulation of such a view depended on and derived from well-documented case-studies that attempted to comprehend the essential features of criminal justice as a whole, albeit in the context of particular local settings (see, for example, Blumberg, 1967; Emerson, 1969; Cole, 1973; Neubauer, 1974; Bottoms and McClean, 1976). If any conception of justice could be said to characterize the bureaucratic organization of the criminal courts it would be a *routinized justice* concerned above all with getting through each day's crowded court lists as efficiently as possible. It is difficult to be certain how far an inherent practical cynicism and absence of any more elevated moral sense of justice contributes to the dominance of the 'production ethic' or how far the pressures for administrative survival create cynicism and devalue the concepts of justice held by the professionals concerned. The net result, however, is a closed system of bargaining and negotiated justice, with only the occasional 'special case' to give a show of more open and truly adversarial justice, in which the interests of the defendant are matched against those of the community in open court.

The overwhelming impression conveyed by first- or second-hand experience of the criminal justice process, as observer or participant, is that of an established set of institutional arrangements involving several groups of more or less permanent actors dealing with an essentially transient group of 'consumers' or 'clients'. Any perceived sense of the system as adversarial resides not in the legalistic ideal of a 'truth-seeking' conflict between those devoted to the proving of guilt and the defence of the innocence of the accused, but rather as between the routine machinery and official personnel, on the one side, and the defendant, on the other. The contrasting images of the organization and the individual, the familiar and the unknown, were well expressed by the authors of a recent survey of criminal justice in an English city:

> To the court administrator, to the judge or magistrate, to the professional lawyer, the court is a familiar place. Familiar rituals are re-enacted daily, often many times a day. These men know with almost unfailing precision what will happen next. . . . No overt collusion to manipulate justice exists; what does exist are the shared understandings of habitués. These understandings may become so routine and commonplace that the habitué forgets that the outsider finds them strange, and often alienative.
> [Bottoms and McClean, 1976, p. 55]

In consequence the defendant is often bewildered by the proceedings and incapable of understanding what is happening to him
(see also Dell, 1971; Carlen, 1976a). Studies of defendants' own
perspectives and their experience in and out of the criminal court
provide graphic examples of their consciousness of 'outsider' status
in an organized 'game', purporting to be the administration of
justice.

The defendant's sense of isolation and cynicism can be particularly acute with regard to his relationship with his own lawyer,
especially if provided by the state. Sudnow (1965) drew attention to
this in his study of the routine handling of cases in a public defender's
office where lawyers worked in close liaison with the prosecuting
district attorney; only the most exceptional case was handled
otherwise than as a 'backstage operation', with prosecuting and
defense lawyers leaving court together 'arm in arm'. So too in
Casper's survey of seventy defendants convicted of felony charges
in Connecticut there was the priceless reply of one defendant to the
interviewer's question — 'Did you have a lawyer when you went to
court?' Answer: 'No, I had a public defender.' (Casper, 1972, p. 59).
The whole procedure was seen as an amoral game with several
subtle twists:

> The gamelike nature of the proceeding extends even to the
> defendant's *own* lawyer, for he is himself playing a game,
> mediating between prosecutor and defendant, pursuing inter-
> personal and professional goals that are seen as contrary to the
> goals of the defendant, whom the lawyer is supposed to be
> representing.
> [Casper, 1972, p. 115]

Finally, a selection of very apt quotations can be taken direct from
the words of defendants interviewed in the study by John Baldwin
and Michael McConville, focusing upon plea-bargaining in England:

> '. . . the barrister who's defending and one who's prosecuting have
> got it pretty nearly sewn up. They're in the law courts every day
> and they know what's going on. They brow-beat many people
> [into pleading guilty.] Where they've got a long indictment, they
> talk between themselves like a couple of carpenters saying "We'll
> cut that piece to that length." It's just a job for them.'
> [Baldwin and McConville, 1977, p. 25]

'The fellow who's prosecuting, and the fellow who's defending

are not really interested in me. . . . After all, they're near enough
mates in the same play. They're the cast of the play, you're just
the casual one-day actor. It's just another day's work for them.'
[Baldwin and McConville, 1977, p. 85]

'Everything in the bloody machinery of the court is against you
from the start. . . . I'm the guy in the middle and who's bothered
about me? I've often thought that, from the accused's point of
view, it's like a guy on a desert island, with all the sharks coming
in for a little nibble. . . . I was just dissatisfied with them all in
general — putting it bluntly, they all basically piss in the same
pot.'
[Baldwin and McConville, 1977, p. 85]

This picture of the daily routine of the criminal courts, in which
the defendant appears to be intrusive, provides the basis for
understanding the bargaining that occurs between the various
personnel. Different professional groups, often with their own
standards and codes of ethics, come together in order to reach
mutually acceptable resolutions of potentially conflicting issues. It
is very much a matter of teamwork, according to ground rules and
an assumed morality of judicial procedure that are taken for granted
(see Sudnow, 1965).

A.S. Blumberg was the first to articulate a comprehensive and
highly critical model of American criminal justice as a 'people-
processing' machine, in which police, lawyers and judges lived and
worked in a 'symbiotic relationship of convenience and necessity'
(Blumberg, 1967, p. xx). The primary orientation was to the
depersonalized goals of production, treating accused persons as
objects rather than as individuals with rights under the rule of law,
to which lip-service was paid:

It is a perfunctory, administrative-bureaucratic version of due
process that has been implemented in our criminal courts.
'Bureaucratic due process' serves as bland obeisance to constitutional principles. It is characterized by the superficial
ceremonies and formal niceties of traditional due process, but
not its substance. . . . The rational-instrumental goals of the court
organization, in its urgent demand for guilty pleas, have produced
a bargain-counter, assembly-line system of criminal justice which
is incompatible with traditional due process.
[Blumberg, 1967, pp. 4-5]

Blumberg claimed that the rules of due process were predicated
upon an *adversary* system of criminal justice, and that they lost

most if not all of their meaning in a contemporary system in which the adversary element had been whittled away by a negotiated justice that denied the vast majority of defendants a proper trial in open court. Among the organizational elements identified by Blumberg as tending to deflect from the prescribed goals of due process and the rule of law were: (1) the occupational and career commitments, in which personal prestige and empire building took precedence over official goals; (2) the unofficial goals of maximum productivity, and the routine of subcultural solutions to achieving such goals; (3) institutionalized evasions of due process requirements; and (4) the pervasive secrecy and relative immunity from public scrutiny (Blumberg, 1967, p. 34). Metropolitan Court was seen as a 'closed community', with accused persons coming and going, but with the structures and personnel remaining to carry on their respective careers, occupational and organizational enterprises.

Similarly, in England, the study by Bottoms and McClean concluded by suggesting a rather toned-down version of criminal justice as a bureaucracy. They favoured a 'Liberal Bureaucratic Model', contrasted with Packer's 'Crime Control Model'. The liberal bureaucrat supported the need for a measure of due process for the protection of individual liberty, but his essential pragmatism made him equally conscious that 'things have to get done, systems have to be run' (Bottoms and McClean, 1976, p. 229). Although crime control should not be the overriding value of the criminal justice system nevertheless the indiscriminate extension of due process procedures should be tempered by the constraints of administrative efficiency. The values of liberal bureaucracy were described as all-pervasive in the actual operation of the English criminal process, from the pressures upon defendants to elect for summary trial, through the 'practical' advice of defence lawyers to their clients to plead guilty, to the built-in deterrents against 'frivolous' appeals after conviction and sentence. The fact that even defence lawyers worked within such a system meant that crucial guarantees of the reality of due process were denied to defendants, and further strengthened its convergence with the Crime Control Model.

As a slight variant upon the bureaucratic image, George F. Cole (1970, 1973) viewed the administration of justice in terms of an *exchange system*. This could be seen as a development of Newman's empirical 'decision-flow' approach, which by emphasizing the importance of the network of relationships among criminal justice personnel, provided a link between organizational constraints and negotiated justice. Cole's analysis derived from a study of work in a prosecuting attorney's office in Seattle, where he was able to observe the close ties that existed between defence and prosecuting lawyers, and between the D.A. and the local community. In particular, there were crucial financial and career incentives for lawyers to cooperate with the prosecuting attorney, who was himself keen to 'reach accommodations so that the time-consuming formal proceedings need not be implemented' (Cole, 1970, p. 340). Thus an 'exchange relationship' developed, which when extended to other actors in the legal system resulted in an interlocking *exchange system*. This view of criminal justice as a set of inter-organizational relationships was an implicit denial of the adversary model, with decisions being the outcome not of a judicial resolution of conflicting evidence in open court but of backstage accommodations. Cole's perspective allowed due weight to be given to the values and aims of the separate professions as well as to the overarching demands of criminal justice as an organization in its own right:

> This view recognizes that an organization has many clients with which it interacts and upon whom it is dependent for certain resources. As interdependent subunits of a system, then, the organization and its clients are engaged in a set of exchanges across their boundaries. . . . The participants in the legal system (game) share a common territorial field and collaborate for different and particular ends. They interact on a continuing basis as their responsibilities demand contact with participants in the process. . . . Exchanges do not simply "sail" from one system to another, but take place in an institutionalized setting which may be compared to a market.
> [Cole, 1970, p. 332]

Each of the official participants in the bargaining process attempts to seek an accommodation that is consistent with his professional values and personal career ambitions, as well as being compatible with the administrative objectives of the organization. In such circumstances, the formal requirements of the law tend to be relegated to an insignificant position in the hierarchy of values, and consequently 'a wide variety of departures from the strictures of the due process model are accepted by the actors in the justice system but are never publicly acknowledged' (Cole, 1973, p. 69). Such widespread practices could be said to constitute 'work crimes', but the shared knowledge of their commission merely served to bind more closely together the members of the criminal justice system into 'an effective network of complicity' like that of each occupational culture writ large across the relations between many different groups (Cole, 1973, p. 69; Blumberg, 1967, p. 70).

The composite image of the administration of justice as a bureaucratic organization striving for administrative efficiency, in which decisions are typically the results of established patterns of accommodation in a system of exchange relationships, provides a plausible if as yet tentative framework for a realistic understanding of much that goes on behind the scenes. Several studies in America have already shown how well this image fits the negotiations that take place between prosecuting and defence attorneys (see, for example, Sudnow, 1965; Skolnick, 1967; Cole, 1970, 1973; Battle, 1971; Neubauer, 1974); and exploratory studies in Britain are beginning to reveal a similar if perhaps less developed state of affairs (see Bottoms and McClean, 1976; Baldwin and McConville, 1977). Throughout all these studies a major emphasis has been upon the nature and extent of the bargaining surrounding the choice of plea by defendants. The Birmingham study of Baldwin and McConville revealed that over two-thirds of their sample of defendants who changed their plea from one of not guilty to guilty, after being committed for trial by jury to the Crown Court, appeared to have been involved in some kind of negotiation (Baldwin and McConville, 1977, p. 27). The fact that the most important factor in these late plea changes was the advice of their own barristers shows how crucial to our understanding is further knowledge of the professional ethics and 'working philosophies' of these key participants. It may be that their advice was indeed in the best interests of their clients, and that other elements in the situation are largely to blame for any 'miscarriages' of justice that may occur, such as police questioning of suspects and judges' sentencing discounts:

> The injustices we have encountered are, in our judgement, essentially the product of a system that gives too little protection to the innocent and too often sacrifices the needs of the individual to the requirements of bureaucratic efficiency. This in turn manifests itself in the adoption of standards of behaviour that, although they may well make sense within a system of values thus warped, are seen by defendants as oppressive.
> [Baldwin and McConville, 1977, pp. 115-16]

* * *

Having surveyed, in selective fashion, a wide range of images of the law in action that have characterized criminological study of criminal justice, mainly in the last two decades, a few important qualifications must be appended lest anyone should gain a misleading impression of the kind of understanding that is beginning to emerge. Although we have charted the 'progress' from the study of disparities to the sociological analysis of negotiated justice, we have dealt almost exclusively with what Doreen McBarnet has termed the 'microsociology' of criminal justice research (McBarnet, 1978). The knowledge that has emerged has been primarily descriptive, and the level of explanation relatively shallow, in terms of theoretical or structural aspects of 'macrosociology'. The role of legal structures, legal rules and the origins of legal doctrine has found little place in most past research (see McBarnet, 1976; Low, 1978). McBarnet (1978) has challenged many of the common dichotomies that have been implicit or explicit in the material surveyed in this chapter, such as 'law in the books' *v.* 'law in action', 'due process' *v.* 'crime control', and empiricism *v.* theory. Although I do not go all the way with her critical analysis of these allegedly false dichotomies, I agree entirely with the tenor of her general conclusions as to the need for bridging the gap between the traditional criminological and the more radical 'sociology of law' approaches to criminal justice:

> For a full explanation of how law is enforced then, substantive law, legal structure, and the state must be added to moods and bureaucracies and face-to-face interaction. . . But bringing law in as an explanatory factor in the operation of criminal justice is not enough. We must examine the assumptions and purposes underlying criminal justice itself in terms of its social, historical and political basis, in relation to class, power, interests and ideologies. . . . The implication is that if macrosociology has to be brought in to explain the operation of the local court, so microsociology must be brought in to explain the system, not to analyse the local bobby but the elite of the state, not the petty administrators but the creators of the criminal justice system, not to turn in scorn from abstract questions of power but to examine the real people constructing and maintaining domination.
> [McBarnet, 1978, pp. 31-2]

Preliminary work has been carried out examining the socio-political origins and influence of the judiciary and the legal profession (Wilson, 1973; Paterson, 1974; Bankowski and Mungham, 1976; Carlen, 1976b; Griffith, 1977), and McBarnet has already broken new ground by her examination of the influence of legal rules in the pre-trial stages leading up to the presentation of cases at trial and police arrest decisions (McBarnet, 1976, 1977). All these are vital areas of study, too long neglected by mainstream students of criminal justice. It is likely that the theoretical perspectives that inform such research and the knowledge that emerges will not only supplement what is already known but may well come to alter quite radically the kind of explanations with which we are prepared to be satisfied. However, in the concluding section of this chapter, I want to supplement traditional approaches in a different direction, by facing more directly than I have done so far the normative issues surrounding the values and principles that we might wish to see informing the basic procedures of criminal justice. This discussion will also serve as a prelude to the examination of the substantive objectives of the application of penal measures in Chapter 4.

DISCRETIONARY JUSTICE AND DEMOCRATIC VALUES

Despite the different perspectives in criminal justice research, there are a number of features which all the main approaches have shared. In particular, there has been a common reluctance to confront the issues surrounding the meaning and implication of an overarching principle of 'justice' permeating the entire process. Instead, the concept of justice has either been uncritically assumed to determine the course of criminal procedures, or been displaced in the face of the informal private justice of different occupational groups, or routinized by the administrative pressures of bureaucracy. Closely linked with this apparent 'retreat from justice' has been the almost universal practice of approaching the study of criminal justice from the standpoint of the official personnel who make the decisions, with the result that the legitimate interests of the defendant and the community have been relatively neglected. The time seems long overdue for criminologists to correct these omissions and make the analysis of justice a major focus of attention, bringing the defendant and the community from behind the scenes onto the centre of the stage on which criminal justice administration has for so long been played out by an official cast. There is no doubt about the problems involved in such a reorientation, as it raises a whole range of controversial matters of principle in a society where there is little general agreement on the subject of crime and punishment; but criminology ought to face the challenges of this task rather than leaving the field open to lawyers, politicians and media-informed public debate.

There are at least three aspects of the concept of justice that are relevant here. In the first place, there is the relationship between the institutions of criminal justice and the existence of social (in)justice in the community at large. The importance of this was expressed forcefully at the beginning of the American Friends Service Committee's Report, *Struggle for Justice*:

> To the extent, then, that equal justice is correlated with equality of status, influence, and economic power, the construction of a just system of criminal justice in an unjust society is a contradiction in terms. Criminal justice is inextricably interwoven with and largely derivative from, a broader social justice.
> [American Friends Service Committee, 1971, p. 16]

This raises issues of such complexity that they cannot be dealt with adequately in a book of this scope, but many would share the view of the authors of *Struggle for Justice* that a resolution of the issues of social justice should take precedence over and determine the shape of both criminal justice and criminology as a whole. The second important aspect of justice relates to the choice of objectives within the existing framework of the criminal justice process, according to which decisions are made as to the nature of sanctions and upon whom they are to be imposed. (This aspect will be discussed in Chapter 4.) Finally, the aspect of justice which will be our main concern here revolves around the appropriate procedures for enforcing the law and administering criminal justice. An attempt will be made to outline a possible structure for achieving a greater sense of 'justice of administration' (see Fogel, 1975), bearing in mind throughout the discussion that this element is essentially subordinate to the resolution of the issues of wider social justice and justice as the formulation of policy objectives. The achievement of *procedural justice* can in no way justify an otherwise unjust criminal process or a wholly flawed system of social control; but neither can wider concepts of justice be achieved without at the same time meeting the demands for just procedures.

Discretionary decision-making, often in situations of low-visibility, has been shown to be at the heart of the criminal justice process. It provides the context for the disparities upon which the empirical-positivists focused most of their attention, and its existence contributed to the development of occupational norms for meting out informal justice without trial, together with opportunities for bargaining and exchange relationships within the bureaucratic organization of the criminal courts. A necessary first step along the road to justice is a clearer recognition of the existence and scope of such discretion at each stage where it operates. There is already recognition at some of the more public stages of the process, where it is often flaunted as a major principle — such as in the judicial choice of sentence, or in the decisions of the parole board to recommend release of prisoners on licence. However, it will be suggested presently that such flaunting of discretionary powers *per se* is a matter of serious concern when not accompanied by a complementary awareness of the need for discretion to be structured by the articulation of standards, the giving of reasons, and the acceptance of certain principles of democratic accountability. There are many other examples of more private confrontations between members of the public and official agents of criminal justice, where discretion has not been so readily acknowledged. K.C. Davis, whose book on *Discretionary Justice* (1969) is a central point of reference in this discussion, illustrated the reluctance of senior police administrators in America to acknowledge the exercise of discretion and the 'selective enforcement' which is part and parcel of the patrolman's daily work on the streets. This apparent refusal to acknowledge anything other than a policy of full enforcement meant that no occasion arose for ascertaining community preferences for enforcement policy, or for coordinating police policy with that of prosecutors and judges (Davis, 1975, p. 53). The solution advocated by Davis was *'selective enforcement, along with truthful statement of it'* (Davis, 1975, p. 69). Such a principle, if modified for application throughout the criminal justice system would not replace discretion but set the scene for the clarification of policies, with the possibilities of increased coordination within the process and increased accountability to legitimate interests outside.

Once the existence of discretionary power has been acknowledged by the decision-makers, the next step is what Davis called the *structuring of discretion*:

> The seven instruments that are most useful in the structuring of discretionary power are open plans, open policy statements, open rules, open findings, open reasons, open precedents, and fair informal procedure. . . . Openness is the natural enemy of arbitrariness and a natural ally in the fight against injustice. [Davis, 1969, p. 98]

In applying his ideas to the practical situation of police decision-making, Davis made it clear that individualization was still a vital element in law enforcement, but it should be controlled by an appropriate mixture of rule and discretion, so that 'the more general the question of policy the greater the rule content of the mix — the more the need for individualizing the greater the discretion content of the mix' (Davis, 1975, p. 158).

Powerful pressures already exist in the United States towards the introduction of rule-making and the articulation of standards, supported by official commissions and professional associations — not only in the sphere of police work but more especially in sentencing and parole decisions. The signs of any similar movement for change in England are much less distinct and altogether more hesitant. Admittedly, there have been a few minor changes involving legislative intervention in court decisions on the refusal of bail before trial (culminating in the Bail Act, 1976), and the Home Office have spelled out guidelines for parole decisions; but these are mere drops in an ocean of largely unstructured discretion enveloping the crucial areas of police policy, sentencing, and a range of other decisions by lawyers and judges in and out of court. Government departments, professional associations, and other quasi-independent supervisory bodies are all equally implicated in this failure to clarify policy and give adequate reasons for decisions in particular cases. Without a determined and genuine commitment to 'opening up' criminal justice policy and procedures, all claims to a system of real justice must ring somewhat hollow and the overall impression must remain one of official arbitrariness and professional caprice.

Before considering the questions raised by Davis' demand for 'fair informal procedures', we must follow through the implications of 'open policy statements' and the spelling out of objectives and reasons for decisions. One obvious consequence of such an opening-up process would be the bringing to the surface of conflicts and disagreements that had previously been concealed, but which would now need to be confronted. Crucial choices would have to be made about the appropriate forum for the attempted resolution of such conflicts as would emerge, but one thing at least is certain — the 'resolution' would no longer lie solely in the hands of single professional groups or be subject to the private bargaining typically found in the current administration of justice. Whatever theory of accountability is meant to inform the criminal justice process all the evidence points to the conclusion that in practice very little meaningful accountability exists. At the end of his essay on discretionary justice in America, Reiss concluded that 'the system of criminal justice in the United States is not generally accountable to external authority', and most organizations (or 'subsystems') within criminal justice were incapable of controlling their internal exercise of discretion (Reiss, 1974, p. 74). The main reasons for this state of affairs included: (1) the lack of any central coordination or control by an organization such as a ministry of justice; (2) the power to detect the improper use of discretion tended to be internal to each organization, with little or no scope for effective control by outside bodies; (3) the control of organizations by professionals who resist the review of the discretion which is seen as being at the core of professionalism; and (4) the bureaucratic nature of the whole operation which insulates it against certain forms of accountability. In fact, in Reiss' view, the very organizational problems inherent in the criminal justice system provided a possible basis for improving its accountability:

> Paradoxically, the solution to structuring and monitoring the exercise of discretion lies in some of the same sources that interfere with holding organizations and agents accountable for their exercise of discretion since legal, bureaucratic, and professional organizations are the major means for the control of discretion. Inasmuch as all of these forms neutralize civic power, it seems essential to develop viable alternatives for civic control of the legal system, whether by civic review, an ombudsman, or

other public systems of accountability.
[Reiss, 1974, p. 74]

Bringing together the various personnel and professions involved in criminal justice at the local and national level might be a start in the right direction towards breaking down some of the barriers of communication and alienation that exist, but the essential message that emerges from this review is that the dangers of injustice that derive from private bargaining and informal procedures must be met by establishing *effective channels of accountability*, to enable a wider public to have a more direct say in the formulation and application of policy. What is required, in my view, is a readiness by all those involved at the various stages of criminal justice to subject their policies to public scrutiny and to recognize much more explicitly than hitherto that the role of the community is central to the entire enterprise rather than being a peripheral hinderance to the smooth operation of an ongoing system. But what meaning attaches to taking 'the community' seriously in such a context as this, in view of the notorious difficulties of identifying any such homogeneous entity in modern life? Firstly, it would involve a reappraisal of the crucial role that individual members of the public play in initiating the procedures of law enforcement by their decisions to report crimes to the police, of which they may have been victims or witnesses. There is already substantial evidence of the influence of the complainant's attitudes upon police decisions to record crimes and take action against possible suspects, whether in terms of arrest, cautioning or prosecution. The work of Donald Black in America has provided the most thorough documentation of the role of citizens in mobilizing the police. He suggested that the typical three-way encounter involving the police, a suspect and a complainant was like a microcosm of the total legal control system, as it personified the state, the alleged threat to social order and the general public (Black, 1971, p. 1,092). Furthermore he pinpointed the essentially democratic character of the pattern of police compliance with complainants' preferences for official action or inaction, but recognized that this brought its own peculiar problems of 'injustice', in view of the moral and social diversity of such attitudes:

While the structure of the process is democratic in this sense, it most certainly is not universalistic. The moral standards of

complainants vary to some extent across the citizen population, thereby injecting particularism into the production of outcomes. There appears a trade-off between democratic process and universalistic enforcement in police work.
[Black, 1970, p. 739]

The active cooperation of victims and witnesses also plays a crucial part in preparing a case for trial and securing an appropriate verdict. Although traditionally the interests of the victims of crime have seemed to be of relatively minor concern to the community in general and as reflected in decisions of the sentencing courts, recent trends suggest a revival of the victim's importance in the introduction of compensation schemes, and the growth of voluntary groups to help crime victims in the immediate aftermath of their experience (Schafer, 1960; Wright, 1977). Victims of crime are members of the community who have a close personal association with the official process, and it seems essential for criminologists to study their experiences, attitudes and characteristics, and to examine the extent to which proper accountability may be said to exist to those most directly involved in this way.

Members of the public not only become involved with criminal justice in a somewhat *ad hoc* fashion as victims or witnesses, but may also participate through a wider range of more structured involvements, officially intended to increase the democratic element of public accountability. In England, the most well-known examples are the long-established institutions of the lay magistracy and trial by jury (although there is also a potentially important lay involvement in membership of police authorities, and prison boards of visitors). Both these institutions have been the object of critical comment and research over recent years, but rarely has their potential value as 'symbols of democracy' (?) been given its due. In the case of lay magistrates, there has been consistent evidence of the essentially unrepresentative nature of their socio-economic backgrounds (Bottomley, 1973; Baldwin, 1976), which has too often been crudely assumed to explain the inequities of the sentences they pass. Criticisms of juries in this country have been more varied, ranging from accusations of 'middle-class, middle-aged' prejudices, to suspicions that juries are too easily swayed by emotional and 'legally irrelevant' considerations (see Kalven and Zeisel, 1966; Cornish, 1971; McCabe and Purves, 1972b, 1974; Walker, 1975). Established institutions of this kind must be evaluated not against pseudo-objective ideals of uniform justice conceived in the minds of researchers, reformers or professional lawyers, but in the light of a careful analysis of the democratic principles they are intended to embody. A commitment to 'democratization' of criminal justice will inevitably involve some sacrifice of uniformity, and this is just one of the many crucial choices that has to be faced:

> When a legal system organizes to follow the demands of the citizenry, it must sacrifice uniformity. . . . A legal system that strives for universalistic application of the law, by contrast, must refuse to follow the diverse whims of its atomized citizenry. Only a society of citizens homogeneous in their legal behaviour could avoid this dilemma.
> [Black, 1970, p. 733]

Just as criminologists have systematically documented the variations in police behaviour in different communities, and the way in which court decisions seem to reflect local attitudes towards the crime problem, so now there is a need to pursue further the basic questions raised by these findings — not assuming that local variations are always 'undesirable', but teasing out the nature of law enforcement and criminal justice in relationship to different communities (and sections of communities) both locally and further afield.

If victims, magistrates and members of juries are significant representatives of the community so also are those persons who are suspected or accused of crime. The demands of justice and 'fair informal procedures' emphasize that *the criminal justice process has an equal obligation to be accountable to those accused of crime.* We have already quoted some graphic illustrations of how defendants perceive the bureaucracy of criminal justice as arrayed against them in a 'conspiracy of habitués'. An elementary aspect of the accountability owed to defendants is to ensure that they are actually aware of what is happening to them at the various stages. The ignorance of suspects and defendants about the typical procedures they encounter and the decisions made about them should not be tolerated in a society that pretends to care about its standards of justice. The few studies in this country that have paid particular attention to defendants' perceptions all tell the same story of ignorance and passivity. Susanne Dell portrayed the bewilderment and confusion of women remanded in custody to Holloway prison, who on being questioned afterwards did not know what bail was, and neither knew when they could sit, stand or speak during the proceedings, nor what had been decided about them by the magistrates (Dell, 1971, pp. 17ff.). Bottoms and McClean confirmed that this picture was entirely typical of the experiences of a large proportion of their sample of defendants, of whom many retreated into an entirely passive role in the face of the confusion, the uncertainty and almost deliberate exclusion from the very proceedings that were of such direct concern to their futures (Bottoms and McClean, 1976, pp. 55-76). As a final example, Pat Carlen's detailed ethnography of justice in London magistrates' courts managed to capture most perceptively the personal reality of the defendant's 'dummy player' role in the proceedings:

> Faced with contradictory information from opposed professionals many defendants yet sense that the 'in group' of court and enforcement personnel close ranks at times when the whole game is threatened by any defendant who steps out of his role of dummy player. As a result, many defendants, especially 'first timers' acquiesce in being 'serviced' by professionals in the hope that they will thereby propitiate those who construct and dispense justice. Victims of several conspicuous logics, they learn at the initial hearing that they are prevented from speaking when they want to, invited or pressed to change their please when they don't want to and always regarded as people who must be spoken *for* rather than spoken *to*.
> [Carlen, 1976a, p. 91]

A further insidiousness that complicates the situation is the fact that some of the formal structures and opportunities for due process and legal representation may not necessarily improve either the defendant's understanding of what is going on or indeed always improve his ability to struggle against the system in his fight for personal justice. Doreen McBarnet inverted Packer's (1969) dichotomy between due process and crime control, and suggested that due process is often *for* crime control:

> Judges and politicians may deal in the rhetoric of civil rights and due process but the actual rules they create for law enforcement and the policies they adopt on sanctioning police malpractices are less about civil rights than about smoothing the path to conviction, less about due process than post-hoc acceptance of police activities as justifying themselves. Thus a good many of the practices in criminal justice described as informal perversions of the formal rules are in fact allowed, facilitated or upheld in the formal rules of statute and precedent.
> [McBarnet, 1978, p. 30]

The study of plea-bargaining by Baldwin and McConville showed that lawyers do not always act in a way that is seen by defendants as in their best interests (Baldwin and McConville, 1977). Thus, it seems entirely plausible to claim that some of the very procedures officially intended to improve the quality of justice for defendants in the criminal process instead serve only to compound their sense of alienation and injustice. Inasmuch as the growth of due process also contributes to the sense and reality of criminal justice as an organized bureaucracy, an increasingly vicious circle develops which pressurizes the defendant to go along with the system. All along the line there are built-in 'penalties' for suspects and defendants who choose to act in certain ways rather than others (see Casper, 1972, pp. 77ff.; Bottoms and McClean, 1976, pp. 230-5). The natural desire of all defendants for the proceedings against them to be over as soon as possible clearly influences their decisions (and the advice they may receive) about the wisdom of pleading guilty or not guilty, and whether to opt for summary trial or trial by jury at a higher court. An even more important 'penalty-clause' which surrounds the choice of plea is that of the so-called 'discount' principle that allows reduced sentences for guilty pleas and clearly exerts tremendous pressure on a defendant to forego his right to open trial (see Baldwin and McConville, 1978). On the other hand, the existence of such structural and legal factors in the situation led the authors of an earlier exploratory study of plea-bargaining in England to conclude as follows:

> Changes of plea are the result of a realistic and practical approach adopted by police, defence and prosecution lawyers, judges and, often, the defendants themselves. . . . In short, the cases which involved actual plea-bargaining seem to epitomize the realism of experienced lawyers: that is, the bargain which was struck appeared either realistic or practical having regard to the nature and quality of the evidence, the triviality of the crime, the task of proving it before a jury, the tenor of the social enquiry report, and the consequences of sentencing procedures.
> [McCabe and Purves, 1972a, pp. 26-8]

But realistic considerations of optimum tactical advantage within a specific organizational context have no necessary connection with justice. A way has to be found to break into the circle of bureaucratic and professional constraints, to encourage radical changes in the nature of such penalties so that the exercise of rights and the decisions of defendants are taken on their merits alone and not in the context of likely consequences in an imperfect system.

Until some such breakthrough occurs the legal rules and administrative structures of the criminal justice process will continue to push defendants into passive acquiescence. The reality of the protection afforded by due process procedures either comes too late, as when 'confessions' made to the police jeopardize all subsequent attempts by lawyers to retract what is alleged to have been said, or is nullified by the failure of so many cases to come to a trial, without which the due process regulations of earlier stages become meaningless attempts to ensure justice. Simply to demand increased recognition of the legal rights of defendants is unlikely to make much of an impact; the penalties of the bureaucratic structures, the persistence of crime control values (especially in the early stages of police investigation), and the exchange relationships among criminal justice professionals, all conspire against the defendant's chances of a fair trial. It is owed to the defendant and to the community, on whose behalf the system is meant to operate, to open up these aspects to external review; the administration of criminal justice must be looked at from the point of view of the person wishing to defend himself against the charges he faces, and the occupational practices and professional ethics of all those directly involved must be scrutinized against the yardstick of justice not working convenience. Justice should be seen as the outcome of a three-way process, involving the community, the defendant and the public agents of law and order — not a private arrangement between them and the defendant alone. Areas of discretion must be defined, and the exercise of that discretion structured; overall policies must be clearly stated and criteria for decision-making articulated in ways which allow for public debate in advance of their implementation. Effective means of accountability should be established at every possible stage, so that the community knows and approves of what is being done in its name. The defendant must be kept fully informed of what is happening to him and given meaningful opportunities to participate effectively in the process. Reasons for decisions should be given and the procedures for appealing against decisions should be accessible and fair.

Principles of this kind do not apply to criminal justice alone, but inasmuch as they give expression to important social values they are of special significance in this context because, to adapt Ginsberg's phrase, we are here dealing not only with the 'exclusion of arbitrariness' but, more particularly, with *the exclusion of arbitrary power* over any member of our community (Ginsberg, 1965, p. 63).

CHAPTER 4

Towards the Rehabilitation of Punishment

The Humanitarian theory removes from Punishment the concept of Desert. But the concept of Desert is the only connecting link between punishment and justice. It is only as deserved or undeserved that a punishment can be just or unjust. [Lewis, 1953, p. 225]

The principle of responsibility is not founded on the idea that punishment is primarily retributive or denunciatory. Instead it is acknowledged for the sake of liberty itself. [Rawls, 1972, p. 241]

A cynical view of the achievements of academic criminology during the last hundred years might point to the almost perverse way in which it has seemed bent on reversing many commonsense attitudes and assumptions about crime and punishment. We have seen how many criminologists rejected the ordinary conception of crime as a simple breach of the law, and replaced it with various sociological concepts, based on its moral and normative qualities as distinct from its purely legal characteristics. Similarly, an examination of criminologists' traditional approach to the subject of punishment shows that there has been an equal reluctance to accept the appropriateness of this social response to criminal behaviour. The positivists of the last century expounded a variety of often quite sophisticated views about how society should respond to crime and criminals, but the dominant trend within twentieth-century criminology and penology has been towards substituting the ideal of 'individual rehabilitation' in place of punishment. Consequently,

123

without being unduly unfair, the criminological achievement to date could be summed up as having replaced the popular notions of crime and punishment by the supposedly more progressive and humane concepts of individual pathology and rehabilitation. The main aim of this chapter is to focus upon certain elements within contemporary criminological critiques of penal theory that are at last beginning seriously to question what has been achieved under the umbrella of modern penology.

An outline of the various phases of the development of penal thought since the beginning of the eighteenth century typically sketches an early period based on *punishment as retribution,* which gave way at the end of the century to the classical legal doctrines of the enlightenment thinkers (e.g. Bentham, Beccaria) centred around the *diminution of penalties,* to be fixed according to their *general deterrent value.* The nineteenth century witnessed considerable confusion in the emergence of any single dominant penal philosophy, with the widespread establishment of prisons as major instruments of penal policy during this period adding to the problem of the identification of a coherent policy. The eloquent and stimulating account of the role of state punishment during the eighteenth and early nineteenth centuries by Michel Foucault (1977) suggests that virtually from their inception as places to which convicted offenders were sentenced penal institutions were devoted to a *correctional* philosophy of moulding the attitudes and behaviour of the inmates. There is a persuasiveness in his argument that is hard to resist, but at the same time he seems to be superimposing correctional motives in anticipation of the somewhat later influences of positive criminology. The period between the rise of classical thought and the eventual hegemony of positivism was characterized by a mixture of penal thinking, revolving around *deterrence* of a general and individual kind, with prisons being managed as much along lines stressing segregation, control and individual deterrence as for any more directly 'correctional' purposes. The rise of positivist criminology in the last quarter of the century was associated with a penal philosophy that concentrated on measures for *protecting society* by the prevention of crime. The penal ideas of the early Italian positivists have not received the same close attention as their theories of crime, but they exhibited a number of different strands, ranging from the elimination or segregation of dangerous offenders, to individual rehabilitation and broader based measures of social policy directed at the roots of criminal behaviour in society. Thus, although the emphasis on individual reformation and rehabilitation had something of its origins in Italian positivism it did not come to dominate the academic scene until the middle of the present century. We shall first review current attitudes towards the well-established view of rehabilitation as a major penal objective, before proceeding to a more speculative consideration of the possible resuscitation of aspects of punishment and social responsibility in response to criminal deviance.

THE RETREAT FROM REHABILITATION

In an important article, written in 1959, an American academic lawyer Francis A. Allen set out the main tenets of what he first termed the 'rehabilitative ideal':

> It is assumed, first, that human behaviour is the product of antecedent causes. These causes can be identified as part of the physical universe, and it is the obligation of the scientist to discover and to describe them with all possible exactitude. Knowledge of the antecedents of human behavior makes possible an approach to the scientific control of human behavior. Finally . . it is assumed that measures employed to treat the convicted offender should serve a therapeutic function.
> [Allen, 1959, p. 226]

From this quotation we can see the close relationship between rehabilitation and positivist criminology, deriving from its theories of criminal behaviour, its interpretation of criminology as a scientific enterprise and its approach to the objectives of penal measures. Allen highlighted the growth and widespread acceptance within the American penal system during the previous fifty years of juvenile courts, probation and parole, all of which could be seen as both symptoms and causes of the rise of the rehabilitative ideal. It is easy to understand how a penal philosophy that was associated with such apparently desirable reforms would appeal to progressive thought at the time. What is perhaps more difficult to understand is why there has emerged in recent years such a groundswell of *opposition* to the theory and practice of the rehabilitation of offenders.

Challenges to the hegemony of rehabilitation have come from a number of different quarters, from inside as well as outside traditional criminology, and some of the different strands of criticism that have combined in the attack must be disentangled. By way of preliminary comment, bear in mind that many penal measures that could and were retrospectively coopted by advocates of the rehabilitative ideal may have originally been instituted with different objectives in view, based on principles such as the *separate treatment* of young offenders, the institutional and community *control* of (ex)prisoners, and purely *humanitarian concerns* to provide alternatives to imprisonment.

The first indirect challenge came from the changes of emphasis in the study of the causes of criminal behaviour within theoretical criminology itself (see Chapter 2). Ever since Lombroso's modification of his own early claims about the biological origins of crime, criminology has seen a broadening of the scope of suggested causal factors to include a wide variety of environmental and sociological factors in addition to the individual personality and psychological factors that are most compatible with the rehabilitative philosophy. Even among those criminologists who still stress the important role of the individual offender, there are signs of a change of emphasis away from the so-called 'medical model' of deviant behaviour towards an emphasis on the way different individuals may react to available opportunities and circumstances. Much more significantly, in the wake of attacks by radical criminologists, there has been a major shift away from the study of individual criminals in a sociopolitical vacuum towards the study of crime as legally defined and socially situated. The net effect of these changes has been to undermine the perceived relevance and theoretical validity of one of the basic elements of the policy of rehabilitation.

A second major challenge, resulting in what Allen called the 'debasement' of the rehabilitative ideal, stemmed from the insidious and often hypocritical way in which 'the language of therapy is frequently employed, wittingly or unwittingly, to disguise the true state of affairs that prevails in our custodial institutions' (Allen, 1959, p. 229). Under the guise of therapy and the needs of the individual offender, certain special measures for juvenile delinquents or those covered by sexual psychopath laws were supported on therapeutic grounds which often bore only a tenuous relationship to the practical reality of 'treatment' subsequently received. There was often also an official complacency in justifying extended custodial sentences in order that the requisite 'treatment' could be carried out. Concerns of this sort culminated in the entire notion of the indeterminate sentence coming under attack for its therapeutic pretensions in a situation where not only was hard evidence of therapeutic effectiveness generally lacking (see below) but where indeterminacy created unacceptable tensions for prisoners and their families, providing further scope for discretionary decision-making by the executive and instruments of control within penal institutions. Indeterminate sentences and the individualized treatment model on which they are based have been subject to major criticism in America since the early 1970s (e.g. American Friends Service Committee, 1971; Frankel, 1973). In England a similar if somewhat more muted challenge to conventional thinking about the rehabilitative ideal underlying indeterminacy in sentencing has been raised by Roger Hood, particularly in his lecture 'Tolerance and the tariff' (Hood, 1974b). His main attacks have been levelled at the rehabilitative assumptions underpinning the English parole system (which introduced a *de facto* indeterminacy into an otherwise judicially fixed tariff system of sentencing), and also at the proposals of the Younger Committee, to incorporate a discretionary early release into the community for the second part of a 'custody and control order' imposed upon young adult offenders (Hood 1974a, 1974c; see also the discussion in Bottomley, 1978b).

A final decisive challenge to the rehabilitative ideal was provided by the cumulative findings of a number of international surveys of sentencing and the evaluation of penal measures. The logical development of positivist criminology and penological thought in Britain and America, combined with the growing support for a policy of the rehabilitation of offenders, had resulted in a tremendous investment of money and effort in the post-war period into investigating the *rehabilitative effectiveness* of penal measures. Countless research projects were established in order to assess the comparative merits of institutional regimes and to compare custodial sentences with non-custodial alternatives, either by means of controlled experiments or by statistical matching procedures of groups of offenders (see Hood and Sparks, 1970, ch. 6). In the 1950s and 1960s the vast majority of such research programmes focused exclusively on measuring the effects of sentencing in terms of positive changes in the behaviour of individual offenders, with any changes being attributed to 'rehabilitative' success. The first attempts in America to draw together the results of the many disparate and often methodologically complex studies suggested a rather depressing picture (Bailey, 1966; Logan, 1972). The real stir, however, was created by the more polemical claims of Martinson and his colleagues whose massive survey of penal evaluation studies was nearly suppressed by its official sponsors, in view of the overall negativeness of its conclusions (Martinson, 1974; Lipton *et al.*, 1975). The essential message was clear enough: 'With few and isolated exceptions, the rehabilitative efforts that have been reported so far have had no appreciable effect on recidivism' (Martinson, 1974, p. 25). A lively and at times acrimonious controversy was sparked off in the academic journals, following such a provocative and wholesale attack on so much earlier research (Adams, 1974, 1976; Palmer, 1975). Much of the debate centred round methodological issues, and many critics questioned the extent to which Martinson's data supported his pessimistic conclusions. Those who looked for more positive evidence claimed to be able to find a number of encouraging signs that could fruitfully be developed in future evaluation research of a more carefully framed and perhaps less ambitious kind.

Two important reviews have been carried out by British criminologists. Clarke and Sinclair undertook a review of the existing evidence on evaluation for the Council of Europe, and reached a very similar conclusion to that of Martinson, namely that 'there is now little reason to believe that any one of the widely used methods of treating offenders is much better at preventing reconviction than any other' (Clarke and Sinclair, 1974, p. 58). They questioned the pervasive influence of the 'medical myth', according to which delinquency and crime were seen as symptoms of pathology in the individual, and penal measures were expected to provide a treatment effect comparable to that of prescribed drugs for physical illness. In view of the growing evidence of the ineffectiveness of penal treatment, combined with the rejection of the appropriateness of the medical analogy, the authors called for more attention to be paid to some of the broader questions of penal policy, such as those relating to deterrence, public protection, justice, and economic and humanitarian considerations.

The second review was carried out by Stephen Brody for the Home Office Research Unit. Once again the conclusions of this detailed analysis of nearly seventy studies from many different countries were in broad agreement with the newly emerging 'conventional scepticism':

> Reviewers of research into the effectiveness of different sentences . . . have unanimously agreed that the results have so far offered little hope that a reliable and simple remedy for recidivism can be easily found. . . . It has seemed, therefore, that longer sentences are no more effective than short ones, that different types of institutions work about equally as well, that probationers on the whole do no better than if they were sent to prison, and that rehabilitative programmes — whether involving psychiatric treatment, counselling, casework or intensive contact and special attention, in custodial or non-custodial settings — have no predictably beneficial effects.
> [Brody, 1976, p. 37]

A number of possible directions for future research were indicated by Brody, of which some involved further refinement of traditional correctional methods, by improving the criteria of success or failure and widening the range of institutions and sentences being compared. However, other suggestions went outside the framework of most of the studies whose findings had been analysed, and called for research into individual deterrence and the evaluation of sentences 'according to how far they satisfy standards of humanity or demands for retribution or public protection, or simply in terms of more or less sophisticated analyses of relative expense or social cost' (Brody, 1976, p. 66).

It seems clear that the scene is set in Britain, as in America some years ago, for a radical reappraisal of the basic assumptions underlying our penal policy for the 1980s, in the wake of the loss of faith in the rehabilitative ideal. Although the contribution of criminologists in the past has often been narrowly confined to empirical studies that reflected their methodological interests and were compatible with their value judgements on the desirability of individual rehabilitation, criminology must now widen its horizons beyond the purely empirical and engage in detailed analysis of the objectives and justifications of penal measures on moral and social grounds.

There have, of course, always been other strands within criminology and penal policy, alongside the rise of the rehabilitative ideal, so that in the recent period of its decline some of these other concerns have re-emerged as possible replacements. Furthermore, even though rehabilitation may have been dethroned from its preeminent position as an overall objective and justification for the imposition of penal measures, yet a case can still be argued for retaining it as a legitimate activity, under certain controlled conditions, for offenders both in institutions and in the community. Within prisons, Norval Morris has emphasized the need to move away from associating rehabilitation with the idea of prison as 'coerced cure' in favour of a liberated concept of 'facilitated change':

> 'Rehabilitation', whatever it means and whatever the programs that allegedly give it meaning, must cease to be a purpose of the prison sanction. This does *not* mean that the various developed treatment programs within prisons need to be abandoned; quite the contrary, they need expansion. There is a sharp distinction between the purposes of incarceration and the opportunities for the training and assistance of prisoners that may be pursued within those purposes.
> [Morris, 1974, pp. 14-15]

Rehabilitation programmes could still be available but on a strictly voluntary basis for those who wished to take advantage of the opportunities offered. As long as it were conceived in this way, with no hidden strings attached, there is no reason why rehabilitation should disappear entirely from a penal system of the future that may be modelled on very different purposes.

Two of the principles which have emerged as possible substitute candidates for rehabilitation are those of *incapacitation* and *general deterrence.* Some brief but cautionary observations must be made about these before proceeding to an examination of other principles that have received much less systematic attention from penologists.

At its simplest, 'incapacitation' describes the normal consequences of *any* custodial sentence passed by a criminal court. It involves confinement in an institution for a fixed or indefinite period of time during which society is protected from any further criminal activity, irrespective of what happens to the offender after release. There have always been close links between the principle of incapacitation (however interpreted) and positivist criminology. The part played by early notions of 'social defence' among Italian positivists will be considered later, but the more specific links have been by way of the 'debasement of rehabilitation', to use Allen's phrase, and the continuing concern with the concept of the 'dangerous offender' (see Bottoms, 1977).

Allen (1959) rightly pointed out how rehabilitative objectives often resulted in longer custodial sentences, which in their turn could easily come to be seen in incapacitative rather than therapeutic terms. Similarly, in his comprehensive and dramatic portrayal of the outreach of the modern 'therapeutic state' in enforcing therapy upon all manner of deviants, Kittrie showed that despite its avowedly rehabilitative objectives an equally dominant aim was that of the isolation and control of 'socially dangerous persons' (Kittrie, 1971, p. 42). The 'therapeutic state', a direct offspring of positivist-determinist criminology, had always contained a mixture of social defence and individual welfare considerations, so that no progress could really be made until a clear separation in theory and practice had been achieved between the 'health-welfare-morality' role of the therapeutic state and its social defence role:

> Until we face the issue of the therapeutic state's right to confine even when it cannot treat and develop and implement standards and procedures for such admittedly social-defense measures, we will find progress past the deficiences of the criminal model of social controls either strewn with new dangers to individual liberty or else totally unacceptable to meet the needs of social defense.
> [Kittrie, 1971, p. 400]

In addition to the role of incapacitation in the context of this kind of therapeutic double-think, there has been its further role with respect to those identified as 'dangerous offenders'. Tony Bottoms (1977) has traced the concept of dangerousness as a principle of penal policy from Garofalo's early elaboration of *pericolosità*, through the 'social defence' school of continental Europe (see Ancel, 1965), to its modern revival in special legislation for habitual offenders and the mentally abnormal. Contemporary examples of this concern in Britain include the suggestions of the Scottish Council on Crime (1975) that there should be a new form of sentence to be called a 'public protection order' for the long-term detention of the violent offender, and the proposals of the Inter-departmental Committee on Mentally Abnormal Offenders (Butler Committee, 1975) for a new indeterminate 'reviewable sentence' for dangerous offenders with a history of mental disorder. In addition, a working party set up by the Howard League for Penal Reform and NACRO is deliberating future policy on this very subject (Working Party on the Dangerous Offender, 1977).

The essence of this aspect of incapacitation in relation to the dangerous offender was concisely stated by Bottoms:

Positivism's concept of dangerousness is solely forward-looking, and is based on a clear faith in the success of scientific prediction of the future of dangerous individuals, who must then be treated or, if untreatable, confined.
[Bottoms, 1977, p. 75]

Two essential ingredients of a morally valid and effective policy of incapacitation of this kind would seem to be the possibility of arriving at an agreed definition of 'dangerousness', and an ability to predict correctly the likely future behaviour of dangerous offenders, identified according to the definition. In fact it seems most unlikely that either of these criteria will ever be satisfied, particularly the ability to predict dangerousness with any acceptable degree of accuracy. Most working definitions of dangerousness concentrate upon individual violent behaviour, especially of a sexual or homicidal nature. Not only is this an arguably too narrow definition of what is most socially harmful, but practical experience shows how difficult it is to frame legislation precisely enough to ensure that it applies only to those intended. One of many examples is the English experience with the special sentence of 'preventive detention', which was abolished in 1967 largely in view of its failure in this respect. However, even if agreement were reached on the type of behaviour that society was so concerned about that it was prepared to formulate the necessary laws, any application of such laws in our present state of knowledge about human motivation would result in gross *overprediction,* and consequent incapacitation of numerous offenders incorrectly assumed to be future risks to society.

It is particularly important to recognize the grave limitations in predicting dangerousness at a time when penal thinking in many countries seems to be turning to 'predictive restraint' as one possible solution to the failure of rehabilitation. Attention has been drawn in America and Britain to what Bottoms has dubbed an emerging trend towards *bifurcation*:

Put crudely, this bifurcation is between, on the one hand, the so-called 'really serious offender' for whom very tough measures are typically advocated; and on the other hand, the 'ordinary' offender for whom, it is felt, we can afford to take a much more lenient line.
[Bottoms, 1977, p. 88]

Norval Morris showed how official thinking in the United States during the early 1970s succumbed to the 'seductive appeal' of 'drawing a distinction between the dangerous and the non-dangerous and confining imprisonment to the former' (Morris, 1974, p. 62). It offers the possibility that, at one and the same time, the increasing personal and economic costs of imprisonment as a widespread penal measure can be reduced whilst public fears can be allayed by an emphasis on the residual use of prisons for the 'really dangerous' offenders. Likewise, in England and Wales, there are signs of a similar trend, not only in a number of criminal justice policy statements by the government and leading opposition spokesmen, but in observed trends towards the imposition of proportionately fewer custodial sentences but with a marked increase in the number of very long sentences of imprisonment (Bottoms, 1977, p. 88; see also Home Office, 1977).

Despite the many attractions from a public and political point of view of a bifurcated penal policy that retains imprisonment mainly for the preventive incapacitation of the allegedly dangerous offender, whilst introducing alternatives for the rest, it is impossible to ignore the mounting evidence that the practical consequences of such a policy would involve many more offenders being kept in custody who pose little risk to society (see, for example, von Hirsch, 1972, 1976; Kozol *et al.,* 1972; Wenk *et al.,* 1972; Morris, 1974; Steadman and Cocozza, 1974; Greenberg, 1975; Bottoms, 1977). The dramatic outcome of the case of *Baxstrom* v. *Herold,* (383 U.S. 107) in the United States Supreme Court in 1965 made a major if largely accidental contribution to this aspect of penal research by providing a ready-made experimental test of the degree of overprediction in the sentencing of the dangerous offender. The Baxstrom decision resulted in nearly 1,000 'offender-patients' being suddenly released from secure institutions for the criminally insane to ordinary civilian mental hospitals and (for most) eventually back into the community. Although there have been a number of slightly differing interpretations put upon the data of the follow-up study of the behaviour of the 'Baxstrom patients' in the civilian hospitals and after discharge, it seems certain that the degree of violence shown by them was very much less than was assumed at the time of sentence, and that without the Baxstrom decision many of them would have been kept for hundreds of man years longer in secure mental hospitals, despite being little or no risk either to the community or to fellow patients. It is easy to understand the caution of the courts and the psychiatrists when dealing with violent offenders with histories of mental disturbance; as Morris said — 'the path of administrative and political safety is the path of the overpredicted risk'. Nevertheless, when, as now, we are engaged in a search for greater clarity and honesty in the formulation of penal aims, the state of our present knowledge demands that we reject incapacitation as an appropriate alternative to rehabilitation, in so far as it is based on an erroneous confidence in the successful definition and prediction of dangerousness in individual offenders.

There is another variant of incapacitation to which some of its supporters are attracted. Namely, what has been called 'collective incapacitation', as opposed to the 'selective incapacitation' with which the previous arguments about the prediction of individual behaviour were concerned (von Hirsch, 1972; Greenberg, 1975). The justification of imprisonment on this basis does not depend on the accuracy of any specific prediction of an *individual* kind, but rather on the success by which the containment of whole classes of offender protects the community from criminal depredation (see Bottoms, 1978). James Q. Wilson has put forward a spirited defence of this policy, based on his largely speculative views on the extent to which *recidivists* are mainly responsible for the soaring crime rates (as opposed to the 'recruitment' of new offenders). In place of rehabilitation theory Wilson favours the correctional system having the function of 'to isolate and to punish':

> The purpose of isolating — or, more accurately, closely supervising — offenders is obvious. Whatever they may do when they are released, they cannot harm society while confined or closely supervised. The gains from merely incapacitating convicted criminals may be very large. . . . If much or most serious crime is committed by repeaters, separating repeaters from the rest of society, even for relatively brief periods of time, may produce major reductions in crime rates.
> [Wilson, 1975, p. 173]

Wilson's optimism about the likely crime reduction effects of such a policy makes his views attractive, particularly to those who share the basically rightwing hard-line approach in his thinking about crime and punishment, and who may have a gut-feeling that prison is the right place for criminals without having fully thought through their reasons. Other possible justifications for imprisonment will be suggested later in the chapter, but at this point simply note that an attempt to quantify the protection that collective incapacitation might afford the community, by Greenberg (1975), suggested that with the existing sentencing policy in America less than 10 per cent of serious crime was being prevented by the temporary incapacitation of those currently in prison. This was due partly to the relatively low reconviction rates of parolees, but perhaps more significantly to the low overall rate of imprisonment for serious crimes. The incapacitation effect could be reduced or increased by changes in sentencing policy or law enforcement, but for Greenberg, and for me, the implications of empirical findings of this kind suggest the need for a more radical reappraisal of the future use of imprisonment in penal policy, based on the assessment of an appropriate (i.e. just) punishment for an offence of particular seriousness, rather than simply a result of a utilitarian calculation.

Incapacitation as a penal aim can be traced back to the early days of positivist criminology, with the result that its recent renaissance suffers from the taints of positivism; but *general deterrence,* on the other hand, flourished in the period of the classical enlightenment in penology at the turn of the eighteenth century, so that its continued popularity has tended to be strengthened by current flirtations with the notion of a 'neo-classical' revival within criminology. The emphasis placed upon deterrence by the classical penal theorists was not grounded in the range of empirical findings available to contemporary students, but based on a more subjective faith in the power of the law to influence human behaviour. It also drew considerable strength from its underlying element of *retributive apropriateness,* in the determination of the severity of specific (deterrent) sentences.

There are a number of problems and paradoxes surrounding current research and debate about the general deterrent effects of penal measures, which combine to make it one of the most difficult aspects of penal policy on which to reach firm conclusions. The rapid growth in empirical data and comparative surveys of the state of knowledge might seem to suggest an embarrassment of knowledge (see, for example, Ehrlich, 1972; Tittle and Logan, 1973; Antunes and Hunt, 1973; Zimring and Hawkins, 1973; Andenaes, 1974; Gibbs, 1975). Most commentators are in agreement that there are certain circumstances in which the existence of law (and law enforcers) and the severity of penalties are likely to deter people from the commission of crime. Among the commonly cited illustrations of this are the effects of the introduction or stiffening of penalties for drunken driving in Scandinavia and Britain, and the increase in certain kinds of crime in Copenhagen when the Germans arrested the entire police force in 1944! It is also easy to draw on common experience of 'regulatory legislation', whether in terms of traffic flow in city centres or the completion of income tax returns, to support a general belief in the deterrent effect of the law. The question nevertheless has to be posed as to how far arguments and evidence of this sort take us towards the justification of general deterrence as the major aim of penal policy.

The comments of the authors of *Struggle for Justice* summed up the problem well:

> Effective deterrence is the result of the interaction of many variables: the type of crime, the extent of the knowledge that the conduct is a crime, the incentive to commit the crime, the severity of the threatened punishment and the extent to which the penalty is known, and the likelihood that the offender will be caught and punished. The variety and complexity of these variables . . . pose such formidable research problems that it is unlikely we will gain any definitive data, at least for a very long time.
> [American Friends Service Committee, 1971 pp. 56-7)]

The evidence of research and commonsense alike suggests that many types of crime, including many of the most serious to life and property, are committed in such emotional circumstances or with such a degree of premeditation that considerations of deterrence are almost entirely irrelevant — and yet it is often in these more serious types of crime that the courts use deterrent arguments to justify severe penalties. The extent of accurate knowledge among the general public, about crime categories and normal levels of sentencing, falls short of the assumptions necessary to justify a sentencing policy that is sensitive to general deterrence. A consistent theme that runs throughout the history of penal reform, from the rhetorical outburst against the irrationality of capital punishment for more than two hundred offences in England at the beginning of the last century to the statistically sophisticated research of contemporary criminologists, is that certainty of detection is a more likely deterrent than the prospects of the most severe of punishments when (and if) caught. The variety of factors of a personal, social, and purely situational or circumstantial kind associated with changes in the incidence of criminal behaviour is so incalculable that it seems most unlikely that even quite marked changes in the application of the criminal law and sentencing practice would have anything more than a marginal impact on the situation. In any event there seems little grounds in the present state of knowledge to consider general deterrence (in its purely instrumental capacity) as a serious contender to replace rehabilitation, although we shall see presently that there may still be a role for elements of a broader concept of what Andenaes (1974) called the 'general-preventive' effects of punishment.

SOCIAL JUSTIFICATIONS OF PUNISHMENT

An unmistakably negative picture has emerged from this brief consideration of the retreat from rehabilitation. The criminological contribution for the most part has revealed an ethical and empirical bankruptcy that suggests the need for a completely new approach. A further lesson that needs to be drawn is that the language and methods of traditional penology need transcending, and other disciplines brought into the centre of the debate, including philosophy, politics and the sociology of law. Arguably the most significant attempt to reconstruct a positive penal policy, particularly in America during the last decade, has centred on what has been termed the 'just deserts' or 'justice model' (see Bottomley, 1978; Clarke, 1978). Elaborations of the justice model approach to date have been somewhat undeveloped and often inconsistent in their supporting arguments. I want to attempt to relate justice model thinking to a number of disparate trends identifiable in penal philosophy. By locating this new approach within broader trends of penal thought I hope to be able to suggest the outlines of an integrated social justification of punishment.

The formative period of the development of justice model ideas in the United States was the five years between the publication of the American Friends Service Committee's report *Struggle for Justice* in 1971 (significantly the year of the Attica Prison uprising) and the report of the Committee for the Study of Incarceration, *Doing Justice: the Choice of Punishments,* in 1976 (von Hirsch,

1976). David Fogel is usually credited with the coining of the phrase 'justice model' in this context. He was Commissioner of Corrections in Minnesota from 1971-3, and developed his ideas at the practical as well as the theoretical level in the day-to-day running of prisons in Minnesota (see Fogel, 1975; Kwartler, 1977). A major focus of advocates of the justice model was, at the procedural level, upon the need to control the exercise of discretion and to introduce a greater degree of openness and accountability in criminal justice decision-making (American Friends Service Committee, 1971; Fogel, 1975; also see Chapter 3). There was an almost total rejection of the individualized treatment model as the basis for penal policy, but less unanimity on what should replace it as the basic penal objective (to complement the *just procedures* and the programme of '*justice-as-fairness*' in the criminal process). Morris placed the concept of *desert* at the centre of his strategy for the future of imprisonment, by which he meant that 'no sanction greater than that "deserved" by the last crime or series of crimes for which the offender is being sentenced should be imposed' (Morris, 1974, p. 73). However, it became clear that Morris' view of desert was little more than conventional 'limiting retribution' whereby no penal sanction should exceed what was 'deserved', even on the grounds of rehabilitation or the protection of the community. He saw a place for the usual wide range of (often conflicting) objectives, and the only condition he attached was that they should not exceed the deserved maximum (Morris, 1974, p. 75).

It was left to what many regard as the definitive statement of the justice model, the von Hirsch report *Doing Justice: the Choice of Punishments,* to elaborate further upon this central concept. Although they related their ideas to arguments used by Kant and Beccaria, often taken out of context, the authors based their main principle of 'commensurate deserts' on commonsense notions of equity and fairness. Unlike the principles of deterrence and social defence it ensured that the rights of persons punished were not unduly sacrificed for the supposed good of others in the cause of crime prevention. In the choice of penal measure regard should be paid retrospectively to the seriousness of the crime, involving a consideration of the two elements of actual *harm* done, and the extent of the offender's *culpability* (von Hirsch, 1976, pp. 69-71). Unlike Morris' use of the concept of desert, as merely setting an upper limit to permitted punishment, the Committee for the Study

of Incarceration made it clear that its principle debarred dispro-
portionate leniency as well as excessive severity. Even more
significant was their claim that it should have priority over other
objectives:

> We think that the commensurate deserts principle should have
> priority over other objectives in decisions about how much to
> punish. The disposition of convicted offenders should be com-
> mensurate with the seriousness of their offences, even if greater
> or less severity would promote other goals. For the principle, we
> have argued, is a requirement of justice, whereas deterrence,
> incapacitation and rehabilitation are essentially strategies for
> controlling crime.
> [von Hirsch, 1976, pp. 74-5]

Although, in my view, the Committee was not always consistent
in the way it handled the supporting arguments for its case, it does
provide us here with a clear expression of principles to form the
basis for further discussion. In particular it linked the basic idea of
'desert' to the requirements of justice, which was clearly proposed
as a desirable value and goal in its own right, as distinct from the
traditional instrumental justification of penal objectives, such as
deterrence or rehabilitation, in terms of crime prevention and
control. The support for a movement 'back to justice' was admittedly
an unhappy conclusion to which the Committee was drawn by their
interpretation of the existing state of knowledge — 'our solution is
one of despair, not hope . . . what we offer are partial solutions,
while awaiting more insights, greater knowledge, and more complete
answers in some hoped-for future' (von Hirsch, 1976, p. xxxix).
There are others whose response to the pessimistic message of
current evaluation research has not been to look for some other
justification for retaining penal sanctions but to advocate a more
truly radical policy of 'non-intervention' (see Schur, 1973).

Before reaching any final judgement on the merits of the justice
model as so far articulated, the task must be attempted of locating
and thereby developing some of the ideas it contains within the
broader context of penal thinking about the role of punishment in
society. There seem to be at least three strands of thought that offer
possible links between traditional penal philosophy and a more
elaborated contemporary version of the justice model. I have
provisionally identified these as (1) *defensive retaliation,* (2) a
'moralization' (or morale-supporting) *function,* and (3) *social
accountability.*

Defensive retaliation Since the earliest days of social organization
and regulated community life, it would appear that an almost
instinctive response to deviant behaviour has been the banishment
or elimination of the offending member. Even when societies
became more 'developed', and complex structures emerged for the
formulation and enforcement of the criminal law, the same underlying themes were present at the local and national levels, with
transportation playing a major role in English penal policy until the
beginning of the nineteenth century when it was complemented by
the policy of elimination inherent in capital punishment statutes.
Banishment found a place in Beccaria's philosophy:

> Anyone who disturbs the public peace, who does not obey the
> laws, that is, the conditions under which men agree to support
> and defend one another, must be excluded from society — he
> must be banished from it.
> [Beccaria, 1764, XVII, trans. by Paolucci, 1963, p. 53]

It is, however, when we examine the penal observations of the
Italian school of positivist criminology that we find the clearest
attempts to outline a justification for punishment on the basis of
society's retaliation for purposes of self-defence.

Lombroso seemed very uncertain about the appropriate penal
philosophy that could be derived from basic positivist theories of
criminal behaviour, and found a place for a variety of justifications.
To the extent that crime was 'a fatal consequence of certain
constitutions which are naturally predisposed to it' he admitted that
it was, in those circumstances, almost irremediable (Lombroso,
1918, p. 245). In more general terms, he favoured attempts to
prevent, rather than repress, crime, and supported Ferri's idea of
'penal substitutes', which were general social measures aimed at the
sources that gave rise to much crime; but even here he admitted
that 'measures for the prevention of crime are unhappily, with our
race at least, a dream of the idealist' (Lombroso, 1918, p. 331), so
that he felt it necessary to consider the role of existing penal
measures, particularly that of imprisonment. It was in the course of
doing this that he reached the conclusion that society's resistance to
crime was as natural and as necessary as crime itself: 'I do not
believe that any theory of punishment has a sound basis except that
of natural necessity and the right of self-defense' (Lombroso, 1918,

p. 379). In support of this view he cited an impressive roll-call that included Bentham, Hobbes, Beccaria, Ferri, Garofalo, Feuerbach and many other eminent European scholars spanning several generations. In some of his writings Lombroso appeared to reject the ideas of reformation and deterrence, not just (predictably) for 'born criminals', but for other classes as well. Nevertheless, his final thoughts on the question favoured the more conventional positivist philosophy of the reform of the individual offender by the indeterminate sentence (Lombroso, 1918, pp. 385ff.).

Enrico Ferri presented a more consistent framework in his analysis of penal sanctions, grounded in a fairly basic 'social defence' view of punishment, but extending into a more sophisticated view of the role of law in society (to which we shall return later, in our discussion of 'social accountability'). He identified four 'evolutionary phases of law': the primitive (defensive and vindictive reaction), the religious (divine vengeance), the ethical (mediaeval penitence) and the juridical (classical school). Ferri believed that in many crucial areas of intellectual life, including science and the law, society was still at the juridical phase, and in the 'ethico-legal' phase of punishment. The time was then ripe, in his view, to inaugurate the social phase, which, based on new data of criminal anthropology and the statistics of crime, would involve a variety of preventive and repressive social measures to protect society from the assaults of crime (Ferri, 1917, pp. 317-18). A central element in this new phase of law would be the recognition of the punitive agency as a function, purely defensive or preservative of society (Ferri, 1917, p. 321); he rejected the old retributive notion of *lex talionis,* and proudly termed his new notion one of 'defensive vengeance'. The necessity of the legal system gave society the right to punish, so that society punishes crime in order to preserve the legal system existing at a given historical moment:

> Maintenance of the legal system is the exact equivalent of maintenance of society, because society and law are correlative and interchangeable terms. Whoever says law says society, for no law exists without society as no society exists without law.
> [Ferri, 1917, p. 327]

As the third representative of Italian positivist criminology, Garofalo's penal philosophy was closely linked to his theory of 'natural crime', which was seen as an offence against the communal 'moral sense' and a clear indicator of the offender's lack of 'adaptation' to the society in which he found himself. Therefore, the logical social response to criminal behaviour was expulsion or elimination:

> If, by the violation of rules of conduct regarded as *essential,* a member has incurred the reprobation of the class, order or association to which he belongs, the reaction always assumed an identical form, namely, expulsion. . . . The reaction consists in the *exclusion* of the member who is shown to be deficient or lacking in adaptation to the conditions of the environment.
> [Garofalo, 1914, pp. 218-19]

Garofalo recognized the need for relative degrees of exclusion, up to and including the ultimate form of exclusion represented by the death penalty. Transportation was the main form of permanent expulsion, but for young offenders and other appropriate cases Garofalo favoured *temporary exclusion of the offender from his particular social situation* (Garofalo, 1914, p. 225).

The second main element in Garofalo's approach to penal theory was the concept of reparation, with which we shall be dealing in more detail below. In an important section of his treatise on *Criminology,* he examined different concepts of punishment, claiming that although it commonly appears that the aim of punishment is retributive 'social vengeance', yet 'what society actually desires is, first, to exclude the criminal from its midst, and, secondly, to compel him as far as possible to repair the evil which his offense had occasioned' (Garofalo, 1914, p. 230). He went on to emphasize that the policy of exclusion was in no way dependent upon any direct consideration of social utility; in fact, the justification for it developed in Garofalo's thinking from a natural response to 'an inassimilable individual' into the sphere of 'moralization', that we have identified as a second aspect of relevance to the justice model.

'Moralization' function Although very few criminologists have followed up Garofalo's concept of 'natural crime', with its basic underpinning in the moral sentiments of society, there have been some scattered attempts to understand punishment from the perspective of the moral sentiments of its law abiding members. A. C. Ewing developed ideas that had much in common with those of Ferri and Garofalo. Ewing believed that punishment was necessary for the 'self-defence' of society against crime, because the existence of society (or, more specifically, the state) depended on laws and 'a

law that is not enforced by punishment, if necessary, will not be regarded as a law' (Ewing, 1929, p. 47). In an ideal society the laws would always be obeyed without punishment, but the reality of contemporary society is not like this and law implies punishment for those who break it. He recognized that an emphasis upon the moral element in punishment was difficult to disentangle from other concepts of punishment particularly deterrence, but insisted that a distinction should be drawn. Similarly, Ewing's own statements of the role of punishment as 'moral education' were often couched in terms of the 'declaratory' or 'denunciatory' principle:

> The community must defend itself against the violation of its laws, otherwise they would not be laws. . . . The neglect to punish will have consequences that are morally harmful. It will tend to make some people think that lawlessness does not matter. . . . In particular, to punish an act implies a declaration that the act is bad, and the declaration of the State as to certain acts being bad enough to call for more or less punishment must have an effect on the moral standard of the community.
> [Ewing, 1929, pp. 94-5]

One of the difficulties in accepting the approach of Garofalo and Ewing is their assumption of the 'immorality' of crimes themselves, and their failure to distinguish between the effects of punishment (or impunity) upon support for the moral values implicit in specific criminal behaviour and its effects on the general moral support for the law, whatever its 'moral content'. What is at issue, in my view, is not the *morals* of criminals but the *morale* of non-criminals — hence the rather clumsy concept of 'moralization' to describe an effect that may be seen to counteract demoralization among the law-abiding if the offenders are seen to go unpunished.

The 'moralization' function of punishment has no clear-cut identity in most discussions of penal objectives. Inasmuch as it is separately identified, it tends to be associated with the theory of 'denunciation'. In recent years, however, a similar element has become incorporated in discussions of deterrence theory, due especially to the writings of Scandinavian criminologists such as Johannes Andenaes (see the collected articles in Andenaes, 1974). Andenaes preferred not to think about punishment in terms of deterrence, as a simple undifferentiated concept, but rather of the 'general preventive effects' of law enforcement and penal measures, which included (1) the deterrent (i.e. intimidatory) effect, (2) the strengthening of moral inhibitions, and (3) the encouragement of habitual law-abiding conduct (Andenaes, 1952). He believed in the 'moral' or 'educative' value of punishment, whereby punishment is an expression of society's disapproval of the act, and explicitly linked this to the demoralizing effects of criminal impunity by his claim that 'the penalty neutralizes the demoralizing consequences that arise when people witness crimes being perpetrated' (Andenaes, 1974, p. 36). His perspective was nevertheless essentially utilitarian, in that he stressed the crime-preventive aspects of this process, by virtue of the support to the moral inhibitions of the individuals; in other words, counteracting potential demoralization was not seen as a desirable end in itself but as a means of inhibiting the risk of future crime in the community.

The two most recent comparative studies of deterrence (Zimring and Hawkins, 1973; Gibbs, 1975) include brief consideration of this less traditional aspect of the subject. Zimring and Hawkins considered the 'educative-moralizing' function of punishment almost exclusively from an instrumental point of view, and suggested several ways in which it might operate to prevent criminal behaviour. In addition they recognized the importance of the moralization function in strengthening respect for the law:

> If the commands of a legal system were not reinforced with the threat of punishment, many individuals would see no basis for believing that the legal system really meant what it said. . . . Even those who are themselves law-abiding can be demoralized by watching law breakers escape unpunished. . . . The imposition of punishment is a demonstration to society as a whole that that legal system is serious in its attempt to prohibit criminal behaviour: punishment is the convincer.
> [Zimring and Hawkins, 1973, p. 87]

Jack P. Gibbs' sophisticated analysis of the definitional, theoretical and operational aspects of traditional deterrence theory reached conclusions that were very similar to those of Andenaes. It seemed to Gibbs that no adequate theory of deterrence, as such, had been or was ever likely to be formulated, so the situation seemed to demand 'the formulation and test of a theory about the *general preventive consequences of punishment,* which is more inclusive than deterrence' (Gibbs, 1975, p. 219). Among the possible effects examined by Gibbs were what he called 'enculturation' and 'normative validation'. Enculturation (or socialization) was 'the process by which individuals acquire knowledge of and respect for norms, legal or extralegal' and was furthered by instances of criminal acts being punished (Gibbs, 1975, pp. 68-9). The related concept of normative validation was 'the maintenance or intensification of an evaluation of conduct through experience of punitive reactions to contrary acts'. To the extent that these processes had a direct influence upon behaviour as well as knowledge and attitudes, the possible consequences could be increased conformity to the law in a manner independent of deterrence:

> Individuals refrain from illegal acts not because they fear punishment but because they evaluate the acts negatively, and legal punishments maintain or intensify these negative evaluations. Stated another way, individuals have internalized the norm that the law expresses and legal punishments contribute to that internalization.
> [Gibbs, 1975, p. 80]

In order for the moralization function to be integrated into justice model thinking, it would seem necessary to play down its role as emphasized by deterrence theorists and emphasize instead its 'expressive' functions within the social group. Thus Moberly laid great stress upon the *symbolic* aspects of punishment, in the way it marked society's disapproval. Crime creates a bad precedent which punishment must counteract in a 'ceremonial act' of social denunciation:

> There is incumbent on society an attitude towards the wrongdoing of its members which, even at its mildest, takes the form of blame and condemnation. The officers of justice — policeman, magistrate and prison officer or hangman — do for the community something of the work of a town-crier. . . . The punishment therefore . . . is a means by which society sets the stamp of its disapproval on the crime. It is inevitably painful to the person on whom it is inflicted; but its primary purpose is not merely to intimidate the offender or to deter other persons from repeating the offence. It is rather declaratory and educational.
> [Moberly, 1968, pp. 209-10]

Similar conceptions of punishment are found, although not expressed with quite the picturesqueness of Moberly's turn of phrase(!), in recent works by philosophers of law such as Feinberg and Ross. Ross saw the *expression of disapproval* and consequent reproach aimed at the violator as the central aspects of punishment, which he conceived as essentially 'suffering and disapproval' (Ross, 1975). Feinberg described the 'expressive function' of punishment in terms very reminiscent of the writings of Moberly, whereby 'punishment is a conventional device for the expression of attitudes of resentment and indignation, and of judgements of disapproval and reprobation' (Feinberg, 1970, p. 98). He also stressed the symbolic significance of penal sanctions, in which he recognized the very real possibility of punishment not of 'vindictive resentment' (Feinberg, 1970, p. 100). Thus, in his view, the *condemnation* implicit in the application of the law was a fusing of *resentment* (i.e. feelings of revenge) and *reprobation*:

> What justice demands is that the *condemnatory aspects* of the punishment suit the crime, that the crime be of a kind that is truly worthy of reprobation. . . . Given our conventions, of course, condemnation is expressed by hard treatment, and the degree of harshness of the latter expresses the degree of reprobation of the former. Still, this should not blind us to the fact that it is social disapproval and its appropriate expression that should fit the crime, and not hard treatment (pain) as such. Pain should match guilt only insofar as its infliction is the symbolic vehicle of public condemnation.
> [Feinberg, 1970, p. 118]

Social accountability The final aspect to be considered in this review of possible reformulations of the justice model focuses upon the role of law in the regulation of social behaviour, and its implications for the individual offender's accountability to the community. There are obvious parallels with the ideas of the 'social contract' widely debated in the eighteenth century and experiencing something of a revival since John Rawls' *Theory of Justice* (1972). However, the most explicit statements of this position are to be found in the writings of academic lawyers. As so often of course, Ferri has something relevant to say! In his view, law not only had a general defensive role (usually in the interests of the dominant class) but also fixed the rules of conduct that made possible the coexistence of members of society, thereby contributing at one and the same time to social solidarity as well as to social and political inequality (Ferri, 1917, p. 330). In his discussion of the justification of punishment, having established that society had a natural right of self-preservation, Ferri claimed that the basic foundation of law enforcement and penal sanctions was the principle of *social accountability* (Ferri, 1917, p. 360). Man is not only materially but also legally responsible for his acts by the mere fact that he lives in society with other men, and it is this that is the sole source of man's rights and also of his duties:

> He is legally, that is, socially, accountable or responsible for his actions . . . only because, from the moment that he lives in society, every one of his acts produces effects, both individual and social which rebound from the surrounding society upon the individual himself. . . . Every man is always responsible for every anti-juridical act performed by him, solely because and in the measure that he lives in society.
> [Ferri, 1917, p. 363]

Ferri's concern was focused particularly on the nature of responsibility in the individual offender. It is when the concern shifts towards the rest of society that these ideas have a particular message for contemporary advocates of a justice model approach to punishment. The message has come most effectively from lawyers and philosophers of law who are as much concerned with liberty and freedom as with punishment. Henry Hart's essay on 'The aims of the criminal law' represented an influential attempt to understand punishment as an issue of social justice and a direct consequence of the conditions of communal life. According to Hart, criminal law should be viewed in the context of the purposes of law as a whole, which was to enable man 'to realise his potentialities as a human being through the forms and modes of social organization' (Hart, 1958, p. 409); the criminal law defines the minimum conditions of man's responsibility to his fellows and holds him to that responsibility:

> The core of a sound penal code . . . is a statement of those minimum obligations of conduct which the conditions of community life impose upon every participating member if community life is to be maintained and to prosper — that is, of those obligations which result . . . from the objective facts of the interdependencies of the people who are living together in the community and of their awareness of the interdependencies.
> [Hart, 1958, p. 413]

His namesake, Professor H.L.A. Hart further elaborated this concept of law, as deriving from and facilitating the mutual obligations of social living. There is an implicit socio-legal contract, whereby society can be viewed as '*offering* individuals including the criminal the protection of the laws on terms which are fair, because they not only consist of a framework of reciprocal rights and duties, but because within this framework each individual is given a *fair* opportunity to choose between keeping the law required for society's protection or paying the penalty' (Hart, 1968, p. 23). Hart's often quoted definition states that the primary task of the criminal law 'consists simply in announcing certain standards of behaviour and attaching penalties for deviation, making it less eligible, and then leaving individuals to choose' (Hart, 1968, p. 23). This is a method of social control directed at maximizing the freedom of the individual, especially in the way it enables people to make their own decisions and choices of how to live, in the knowledge of what the law punishes and what they can expect to be able to do with little or no interference from such external sources.

The justification of punishment for the sake of greater individual freedom can only be valid under certain types of legal systems and within certain socio-economic structures. Legal systems must be entirely open in their advance announcement of prohibited conduct, and society must be organized in such a way that each individual really does have a fair and equal opportunity to choose between keeping or breaking the law. When, and if, these conditions are met the success of the law can be judged in terms of the promotion of liberty, as advocated by Rawls:

> The principle of [penal] responsibility is not founded on the idea that punishment is primarily retributive or denunciatory. Instead it is acknowledged for the sake of liberty itself. Unless citizens are able to know what the law is and are given a fair opportunity to take its directives into account, penal sanctions should not apply to them. This principle is simply the consequence of regarding a legal system as an order of public rules addressed to rational persons in order to regulate their cooperation, and of giving the appropriate weight to liberty.
> [Rawls, 1972, p. 241]

We are now in a position to suggest a reformulation of the 'just deserts' model of punishment, to meet some of the criticisms levelled against it and, more specifically, to present a rationale for imprisonment in contemporary penal policy.

At the outset it must be admitted that many criminologists and penal reformers who currently favour the justice model perspective do so, as it were, on the rebound from a sudden and often painful realization that the rehabilitative ideal is seriously flawed at a number of levels. This present critique of the justice model is itself partly based on a disenchantment with the ability of traditional penological research to deliver the goods in terms of the rehabilitative effectiveness of penal measures, and is sustained by a grounded scepticism in the likelihood of any dramatic reversals of present negative trends in the foreseeable future.

One of the limitations of the justice model has been its focus on the individual offender and his just deserts to the exclusion of considerations of punishment and justice in a broader social context. Individual rehabilitation is in danger of being replaced by a purely individualistic version of retribution. The development of a framework for the individualization of punishment is indeed a key element in our reformulation, but the concept of 'just deserts' also needs extending in the direction of a more 'socially justified' philosophy of punishment. Social justification of the kind envisaged lies not mainly in terms of utilitarian objectives of crime control or prevention, but in a return to some of the basic principles surrounding the origins and organization of criminal law and punishment. The focus is not only on the individual offender but equally on the other members of society, for whom law can provide some sort of guarantee of their 'legal security' from undue state intervention (see Ross, 1975, ch. 3):

> People ought in general to be able to plan their conduct with some assurance that they can avoid entanglement with the criminal law. . . . It is precisely the fact that in its normal and characteristic operation the criminal law provides this opportunity and this protection to people in their everyday lives that makes it a tolerable institution in a free society. Take this away, and the criminal law ceases to be a guide to the well intentioned and a restriction on the restraining power of the state. Take it away is precisely what you do, however, when you abandon culpability as the basis for imposing punishment.
> [Packer, 1969, pp. 68-9]

For law to have this essentially liberating role not only must there be clear and open statements of the content of law, but its enforcement must be seen to be as fair and as sure as possible. If not, the sense of injustice will increase among offenders and non-offenders alike, and widespread demoralization occur in the face of crime unpunished or punished inappropriately. We may grant that legal punishment has a strong moral element and is based on the 'expression of disapproval' but this disapproval may be directed just as much at *the fact of law-breaking* as at the moral qualities of the illegal behaviour in question.

The real test of a fully-fledged justice model comes when its practical viability is considered in relation to the mechanics of sentencing and the choice of specific penalties. In its elaboration of the principle of 'commensurate deserts' the Committee for the Study of Incarceration identified *harm* and *culpability* as the two basic elements in the assignment of the seriousness of an offender's crime (von Hirsch, 1976, pp. 69-71). In a heterogeneous society subjective evaluation of 'harm' will vary according to any number of social, economic and personal variables, and the interpretation of 'culpability' takes on a substantially changed complexion if there exists a genuine awareness of inequalities of opportunities and injustice within the social structure. Roger Hood has called for a re-drawing of the 'crime-punishment equation', based on a moral and social reassessment of the seriousness of crime and the harm done (Hood, 1974b, pp. 5-7):

> The new approach addresses itself directly to the moral evaluations of these judges and the way they interpret the gravity or dangerousness of various offences in modern society. It does not take judicial opinions for granted and would aim to bring the judiciary back into a critical debate over how our society should define its deviants and what system of punishments are justifiable in a social order still full of inequities and injustices.
> [Hood, 1974b, p. 14]

From Scandinavia, Professor Nils Christie has provided even more challenging support for the idea of criminal courts as clearly defined arenas for moral evaluation and the 'creation of conflict', so that society can become involved in a public debate on the type of morality that should be the foundation of penal measures (Christie, 1974, 1977):

> The courts have for a long time been drifting in a stagnant lagoon protected by the belief that they are, through expertise, striving to reach attainable utilitarian goals. It is time that they were forced out of this and into the flowing waters of a clearly expressed and exposed morality.
> [Christie, 1977, p. 296]

Apart from the resolution of differences between competing evaluations of the degree of social harm posed by specific criminal acts,
the courts have the function of assessing 'culpability'. Within a
reformulated justice model the social and judicial assessment of
culpability must attempt to find room for the *individualization of
punishment,* according to broad criteria relating not only to 'our
understanding of the motivation of the offender and the interactions
in the situation surrounding his act' (Hood, 1974b, p. 6) but also
more problematically to any extenuating circumstances deriving
from the offender's environment or position in the social structure
(Christie, 1974, pp. 293-4). Attempts such as these to take account
of social inequalities in the context of mitigation of deserved
punishments can, of course, be seen as only very marginal gestures
towards the fundamental problem identified in *Struggle for Justice*:

> To the extent, then, that equal justice is correlated with equality
> of status, influence, and economic power, the construction of a
> just system of criminal justice in an unjust society is a contradic-
> tion in terms. Criminal justice is inextricably interwoven with,
> and largely derivative from, a broader social justice.
> [American Friends Service Committee, 1971, p. 16]

It is perhaps not entirely evading the issue to suggest that the
answer to many of the radical critiques of criminal justice and penal
policy is the same as that to many of the misconceptions in traditional
positivist criminology: just as the concept of 'crime' has no monopoly
of what is immoral or socially harmful and penal policy *per se* has
probably little impact on crime rates, so equally the 'solution' to the
problems of social inequalities should not be sought in manipulation
of legal punishment but in a frontal attack on the problems at
source.

Finally, what of the role of imprisonment in this scheme of
things? The inclusion within the justice model of socially-oriented
elements such as those concerned with reciprocal relationships of
community life under the rule of law, and the need to counteract
possible demoralization among the law-abiding, suggests a
philosophy of punishment that draws any integrative power it may
possess from a loose version of the notion of 'social contract'. If this
has any plausibility, then the ideas of 'defensive retaliation' provide
us, in modified form, with a possible basis for justifying the particular

nature of imprisonment as a penal sanction. Drawing upon the penological ideas of Garofalo, we may be able to appreciate the appropriateness of the temporary exclusion of the offender from the community-whose rules he broke, thereby showing himself (at least for the time being) unable to adapt to the social demands of his situation. The extreme penalties of capital punishment and imprisonment for life reflect a total and permanent rejection from society, but other custodial penalties while reflecting a feeling of temporary unsuitability for continued membership of the community on the normal terms do at the same time hold out the prospect of re-entry to the community. In his examination of prison as 'deserved punishment' Norval Morris drew a distinction between 'desert as related to salvation or ethics, admission to the company of heaven or of men of virtue, and desert as related to social organization as it is, admission or re-admission to the company of citizens' (Morris, 1974, p. 73). In the latter context, prison can be viewed as either *rejection* or *expiation:*

> Imprisonment is not now seen as a permanent social rejection; it is at the most a temporary banishment; the prison gates open for all but a very few. Imprisonment is thus, in terms of this distinction, expiative and not rejective.
> [Morris, 1974, p. 74]

Without wishing to get embroiled in the exact interpretation of the concept of 'expiation' (with its theological overtones), we can accept as a possible justification for the future use of imprisonment the idea of *temporary social exclusion,* that symbolizes society's judgement upon behaviour that disqualifies the offender from enjoying the normal benefits of community life. If prison is interpreted as *social disqualification,* then a sentence served can be seen as a measure of requalifying the offender for a place in society. In Foucault's terms, we would be moving towards a general penal philosophy of which the object is to 'restore the juridical subject of the social pact' rather than the correctional positivist aim of 'shaping an obedient subject', (Foucault, 1977, p. 129; see also Bottoms, 1978). Ultimately, therefore, if the application of penal measures is primarily justified in terms of requalifying individuals for membership of society, the implications are more far-reaching than simply the future role of imprisonment. Questions are raised not only about other penal measures but about the function of criminal law in society. It is to these questions that we turn in the final section of this chapter.

RESTITUTION, LAW AND SOCIETY

Our reformulated justice model is now seen to incorporate as a major objective of punishment the requalification of offenders as members of the community, against whose legal norms they have offended. Imprisonment for the minority of most serious offenders may be seen as an appropriate means of disqualification, but for the majority of offenders a choice of sentence is required that will serve as a different form of 'satisfaction' to society for the harm done. Can such long-established principles as *restitution* and *reparation* be integrated into the proposed framework?

The justice model is firmly based on the concept of deserved *punishment,* and to that extent it might appear at first sight to be no more compatible with the concept of restitution than with that of rehabilitation. Traditionally these penal objectives have been seen as mutually exclusive. Thus in his classic formulation of a theory of the evolution of law in society, Emile Durkheim contrasted 'restitutive law' with 'repressive' or 'penal law' (Durkheim, 1893, 1901). Despite the fact that it is now generally agreed that Durkheim's suggestion that as societies become more developed they move from repressive to restitutive law is the *reverse* of what typically happens (see Schwartz and Miller, 1964; Barnes, 1966; Chambliss and Seidman, 1971; Sheleff, 1975; Spitzer, 1975), nevertheless the conventional approach is to categorize legal systems as predominantly either restitutive, penal or rehabilitative. There are, however, some hints from historical precedents and contemporary analyses of the concept of restitution that certain elements of punishment and restitution are not so totally incompatible as has previously been thought.

Historically, restitution to victims of crime in Western European society predated the formal institution by the state of the machinery of law enforcement (Schafer, 1960, 1968). In the form of compensation or 'composition' it served to replace the even earlier response of retaliatory revenge and blood feuds, and was thus mainly applied to private wrongs rather than public crimes. According to Schafer, in some early societies compulsory restitution was imposed not mainly in the interests of the victim but to increase the severity of the criminal's punishment' however, 'it was only toward the end of the Middle Ages that the concept of restitution was closely related to that of punishment, and temporarily included in penal law' (Schafer, 1968, p. 14). A concern for the interests of the personal victim of crime constituted a common element in early procedures for restitution and legal punishment, but it was also the changing view of the legitimate role and definition of the 'victim' that gradually pushed the two concepts apart. The state took upon itself the role of the depersonalized victim and this hastened the rapid decline of the importance of individual victims at all stages of criminal justice and penal policy (Schafer, 1968, ch. 1). The formal and often rather arbitrary distinction between crimes and torts that became established in most modern penal systems further served to strengthen the belief that punishment (for crime) and restitution or compensation (for torts) could not coexist.

Recent years have witnessed a revival of interest in the victims of crime, both within academic criminology with its growth of 'victimology' (see Drapkin and Viano, 1974a, 1974b; McDonald, 1976), and in the introduction of a wide range of practical schemes for compensation and other help to crime victims (see Schafer, 1960). More sophisticated analyses of the role of restitution as a 'new paradigm' within criminal justice and penal policy have been developed (see Barnett, 1977). Many advocates of restitution see it as a purely rehabilitative measure, or what Eglash (1958) has termed 'creative restitution', that brings home to the offender a realization of the consequences of his action. For others its main justification lies in the recompense afforded to the individual victim. However, in order for restitution or reparation to be incorporated into the justice model a different and wider perspective must be adopted. Deserved punishment should be seen to involve a basic restitutive element, aimed at 'restoring the balance' disturbed by the original crime. 'Punitive restitution' of this kind would be founded on an appreciation of the social significance of both crime and punishment. It may be that in some cases an appropriate punishment would involve personal reparation to an individual victim, thereby 'giving the criminal a chance to work his passage back to society' (Schafer, 1960, p. 121), but the basic orientation would be an awareness of the *collective interests* of the community, of which any particular victim is a representative. The revival of restitution and the return of the importance of the victim might signify what Schafer called a new 'universalistic' understanding of crime in place of the traditional 'formalistic-individualistic' orientation in criminal law:

> In past centuries justice was exercised in the name of society, but only the harm or injury to the individual victim was emphasised, and punishment was meted out in accordance with the degree of wrong. In the universalistic orientation of criminal law, on the other hand, the normative organization and value structure of the society in which the criminal and his victim live — and their relationship to this organization and to other members of their group are coming to determine the general perspective of the crime problem. Universalistic criminal law and criminology direct attention to what we tentatively call the criminal's — and perhaps also the victim's — 'functional responsibility', rather than to isolated criminal action or conduct.
> [Schafer, 1968, p. 32]

What is required is not just a new appreciation of the importance of the relationship between the criminal and his victim, but a recognition of the tripartite relationship between the criminal, the victim and society, with general measures aimed at the satisfaction of the community as a whole. Any restitutive concept of punishment in the context of 'functional responsibility' must also find a place for the assessment of society's responsibility for the criminal. A discussion paper of the Howard League for Penal Reform (1977), *Making Amends: Criminals, Victims and Society,* complements its recommendations on making amends to the victim and to society by a novel consideration of the duty upon society in some cases to *make amends to the offender.* This acceptance, in part, of society's responsibility for crime goes some small way towards meeting the radical critique of the tenability of criminal justice in an unjust society, even though any measures would be aimed at the individuals concerned rather than at the wider social structure:

> The amends made by offenders and the amends made to them are never quite separate. Sometimes they are in a sense inter-dependent. . . . Crime is a breach in the relationship between the offender and society — or, more accurately, it is the symptoms of a breach which is often of long standing. If the breach is to be repaired, both sides must play a part in the reparation. *The object at which an ideal penal system should aim is reconciliation —*

reconciliation, that is, between three parties: the offender, the victim and society itself. And reconciliation involves, in one way or another, the making of amends.
[Howard League for Penal Reform, 1977, pp. 14-15]

Are there any grounds for believing that a movement in penal policy towards a justice model based on deserved punishment and social reconciliation through restitution is a likely future trend in the changing conditions of contemporary society?

Durkheim may have been mistaken in his interpretation of historical and anthropological evidence for trends in penal evolution from repressive to restitutive law, but he was almost certainly correct in his theoretical premise that 'the law is the visible outer symbol of the nature of a society' (Sheleff, 1975, p. 45). Largely in response to the stimulus of Durkheim's original formulations, other sociologists of law have analysed the relationships between law and social organization across a wide spectrum of societies at different stages of development. One of the most valuable insights emerging from some of this work is that despite a dominant trend whereby increased social complexity leads to an increase in repressive penal sanctions and a decrease in restitutive sanctions, there are signs of a *curvilinear* relationship that may have real significance for future penal trends (Spitzer, 1975; Black, 1976). In *The Behavior of Law,* Donald J. Black provided evidence that certain social changes in our society may be associated with a decline in the role of penal law, representing signs of a movement back to 'compensating' or 'con-ciliatory' law, and societies characterized by a decline in law of all kind (what he calls, 'legal anarchy'). In examining the consequences for law of increased 'differentiation' or specialization of social function, he found a curvilinear relationship whereby there is less law in societies where people are undifferentiated by function and virtually independent of each other, and also in societies where there is more or less complete *dependence* on other members of society (or 'symbiosis'). Similarly, with 'relational distance' or the extent to which people share in one another's social lives — 'law is inactive among intimates, increasing as the distance between people increases but decreasing as this reaches the point at which people live in entirely separate worlds' (Black, 1976, p. 41). Just as any law that exists in very simple societies, where nearly everyone is close to everyone else, is likely to be remedial rather than penal, so in those

societies that have moved from interdependence to a 'social individualism' there is likely to be a decline in the purely penal function of
law. Black sees these social trends as leading to the return of
'anarchy' — a state of society without law. Communal intimacy is
giving way to situational intimacy, based on the family and friend-
ship, and a degree of *ad hoc* intimacy between strangers; the culture
of the Western world is becoming more homogeneous; social life is
becoming more organized but 'even as this happens, the scope of
organization — the degree to which a group incorporates its
members — has begun to decrease'(Black, 1976, p. 136), with fewer
and fewer people devoting their lives to any specific organization.
Increased mobility has loosened the traditional bonds of social
control, so that 'normative mobility', in and out of respectability,
increases. Black's speculative vision of a society of the future is at
once both pessimistic and optimistic:

> It will be a society of equals, people specialized and yet inter-
> changeable; a society of nomads, at once close and distant,
> homogeneous and diverse, organized and autonomous, where
> reputations and other statuses fluctuate from one day to the next.
> The past will return to some degree, yet society will be different.
> It will be communal and situational at the same time, a unity of
> opposites, a situational society.
> [Black, 1976, p. 137]

In such a new society, he predicts that the role of law will
decrease, even to the point of disappearance. The transitional
period, in which we might already be, may see a return to restitutive
sanctions and conciliatory law, reflecting little common agreement
on the moral values implicit in particular laws but an increased
awareness of the need for the ordered regulation of social life as it
exists. The interests of the individual victim will receive greater
protection, as representing the community, and restitutive
punishment be meted out both as a sign of social disapproval that a
law has been broken and as a means of requalifying the offending
member for re-entry to society.

The Limits of Criminology

*The simplification of the problem of crime to the problem of
the criminal has not paid off. . . . We may have said something
about what should be done with criminals, but we have added
nothing to suggestions for dealing with crime.* [Wilkins in von
Hirsch, 1976, p. 178]

*To attribute an increase in crime to penal policy is therefore
like holding an umbrella responsible for the rainfall.* [Morris
and Hawkins, 1970, p. 116]

Just as Lombroso's focus on the *individual criminal* earned him the
dubious title of 'founding father of criminology', so a central target
of many of the criticisms of traditional positivism has been its
pervasive individualism, not only in its approach to explaining the
'causes' of crime, but also in its tendency to define crime in a
personalized rather than communal way and its apparent faith that
the solution to the crime problem lies in what society does to those
relatively few individuals who have been detected or convicted of
crime. The individual criminal (differentiated from the non-criminal
by a variety of 'pathologies') has been assumed to be a more suitable
focus for criminology's scientific attention than the rather less
tangible elements of social structures and situations that make an
equally significant contribution towards deviant behaviour.
However, by rejecting the conventional 'scientific' objectives for
criminology that have dogged most of its past history, it might
perhaps be possible to reconstruct a more modest but potentially
more valuable and realistic understanding of crime and society's

158

response to it. Traditional cr
ambitious in the objectiv
assumptions, but yet not
and political relativity of
as much in a critique of soc.
(or illusory?) empirical truth.
been conceived and practised a
apparent, but a criminology libera.
dualism and blinkered empiricism has a
of challenge and far from pessimistic.

At many stages in my review I have emphasized the need to spell out the precise questions that research and theory are attempting to answer, so that confusion often disappears by a simple clarification of this kind. Perhaps the greatest need is to keep separate the issues of *understanding* and *controlling* crime. I suggested (in Chapter 4) that traditional penal measures appear to have little systematic or predictable effects upon the crime rate, either in terms of the individuals being 'treated', or the potential offenders in the community; and although the alternative 'justice model' approach to penal policy involves a new perspective upon how we should deal with discovered offenders, it still leaves entirely unresolved the possible policy options for dealing with the roots of crime itself. In his thinking about crime and criminologists, James Q. Wilson outlined a convincing case for the lack of impact of criminological theory upon practical crime control by showing that it was partly due, in his view, to American criminologists' concentration upon individual motivation rather than the material conditions of society, so that 'by directing attention toward the subjective states that preceded or accompanied criminal behavior, the sociological (or more accurately, social psychological) theories directed attention towards conditions that cannot be easily and deliberately altered' (Wilson, 1975, p. 49). He recognized that the more fundamental problem lies in the way *causal analysis* is confused with *policy analysis,* which should start from a very different set of preconceptions than those traditionally found within criminology:

> A commitment to causal analysis, especially one that regards social processes as crucial, will rarely lead to discovering the grounds for policy choices, and such grounds as are discovered will raise grave ethical and political issues. . . . A serious policy-oriented analysis of crime, by contrast, would place heavy

emphasis on manipulation of objective conditions, not necessarily because of a belief that the 'causes of crime' are thereby being eradicated, but because behaviour is easier to change than attitudes, and because the only instruments society has by which to alter behavior in the short run require it to assume that people act in response to the costs and benefits of alternative courses of action. The criminologist assumes, probably rightly, that the causes of crime are determined by attitudes that in turn are socially derived, if not determined; the policy analyst is led to assume that the criminal acts *as if* crime were the product of a free choice among competing opportunities and constraints. [Wilson, 1975, pp. 54-6]

There is an increasing awareness of these relatively new dimensions within criminology, and the need, for certain purposes, to study the 'objective' conditions conducive to crime commission in terms of environment, opportunities etc. (see, for example, Jeffery, 1971; Newman, 1972; Mayhew *et al.,* 1976). However, there are dangers inherent in more overt policy analysis of this kind, including what Jeffery (1971) called 'environmental design' for crime prevention, comparable to those inherent in the practice of the rehabilitative ideal when individual 'treatment' methods may verge on the inhumane. In both circumstances, an overall instrumental aim of crime prevention by manipulating the individual offender or the physical environment can easily cloud the important ethical issues involved in social intervention, both in terms of the justification in its own right of what is being done or in terms of whether the aims justify the means.

We must never lose sight of first principles in our enthusiasm to combat the incidence of criminal behaviour. In the context of crime and criminology the very foundations of definitions and social action depend on value judgements, and the evidence of proven 'effectiveness' leaves little room for complacent optimism. Deviant behaviour that is proscribed by the criminal law, and that proportion of it which results in penal sanctions against individual offenders, encompasses only a small part of what is harmful to society or of what people consider to be morally wrong or socially undesirable. Persuasive arguments can and have been put forward in favour of 'decriminalizing' illegal behaviour that does not appear to harm any 'unwilling' victim or where the consequences of attempted enforcement create more harm and injustice than that which it is intended to cure; conversely, we have seen that there are similarly vociferous

a range of social behaviour to join the list of 'criminalized'
In either situation it is increasingly important to be clear
about the underlying motives and expectations. The definition of
individual acts or social conditions as criminal must be recognized
both in its expressive and instrumental aspects and the implications
of the interaction kept clearly in mind.

The contemporary issues of deviance and social harm are too
complex to be dealt with by simple compartmentalization of this
kind, that is often based on unwarranted assumptions about the
effects of social intervention upon the behaviour of individuals or
organizational structures. It should not be necessary to emphasize
the 'criminality' of a situation before any serious attention is paid to
it. A wider range of labels and actions should be brought into play,
with the role of criminology and penal policy sensitive to the
movements of public concern in different communities at different
times. Social change should not have to wait upon specifically penal
legislation, and the incidence of crime may well be more responsive
to changes in broader social policy. The ideological role of criminology should be clearly acknowledged, with its many and diverse
implications (see Mäkelä, 1975):

> The central criminal-political problems in modern society do not
> circle around *technical* deficiencies or injustices within traditional
> penal law. . . . Under existing arrangements, human responsibility
> is only brought into question within certain sectors of society. . . .
> It may happen that the sanctions of penal law are not so effective
> when it becomes a matter of regulating processes that are really
> central to the society. However, the right to punish and the guilt
> principle are not solely technocratic means for influencing
> behaviour. Penal law is an expression of, and an implement for,
> official societal morals.
> [Mäkelä, 1975, pp. 171-2]

The limits of criminology, as I see them, imply the restoration to a
wider range of academic and socio-political contexts of a shared
responsibility for serious examination of the values and structures
of modern society as they impinge upon deviant behaviour and
other unacceptable conditions of social life. A continuing and
dynamic analysis within criminology of the origins and maintenance
of criminal legislation, the 'explanation' of crime's many facets, and
the values and processes of the administration of justice and penal
policy can help to inform this wider concern which ultimately

places upon society as a whole the major tasks of the necessary social action compatible with the principles it values most highly.

Bibliography

In addition to the works specifically referred to in the text, this Bibliography includes a few other references that readers might find useful.

ADAMS, S. (1974) 'Evaluative research in corrections: status and prospects' *Federal Probation* vol. 38 no. 1, pp. 14-21.

ADAMS, S. (1976) 'Evaluation: a way out of rhetoric' in *Rehabilitation, Recidivism and Research* Hackensack, N.J., National Council on Crime and Delinquency, pp. 75-91.

ALLEN, F.A. (1959) 'Criminal justice, legal values and the rehabilitative ideal' *Journal of Criminal Law, Criminology and Police Science* vol. 50, pp. 226-32.

American Friends Service Committee (1971) *Struggle for Justice: A Report on Crime and Punishment in America* New York, Hill and Wang.

ANCEL, M. (1965) *Social Defence* London, Routledge and Kegan Paul.

ANDENAES, J. (1952) 'General prevention — illusion or reality?' *Journal of Criminal Law, Criminology and Police Science* vol. 43, pp. 176-98.

ANDENAES, J. (1974) *Punishment and Deterrence* Ann Arbor, University of Michigan Press.

ANTUNES, G. and HUNT, A.L. (1973) 'The impact of certainty and severity of punishment on levels of crime in American states: an extended analysis' *Journal of Criminal Law, Criminology and Police Science* vol. 64, pp. 486-93.

AUBERT, V. (1952) 'White-collar crime and social structure' *American Journal of Sociology* vol. 58, pp. 263-71.

BAILEY, W.C. (1966) 'Correctional outcome: an evaluation of 100 reports' *Journal of Criminal Law, Criminology and Police Science* vol. 57, pp. 153-60.

BALDWIN, J. (1976) 'The social composition of the magistracy' *British Journal of Criminology* vol. 16, pp. 171-4.

BALDWIN, J. and BOTTOMLEY, A.K. (eds) (1978) *Criminal Justice: Selected Readings* London, Martin Robertson.

BALDWIN, J. and BOTTOMS, A.E. (1976) *The Urban Criminal: A Study in Sheffield* London, Tavistock.

BALDWIN, J. and MCCONVILLE, M. (1977) *Negotiated Justice: Pressures on Defendants to Plead Guilty* London, Martin Robertson.

BALDWIN, J. and MCCONVILLE, M. (1978) 'The influence of the sentencing discount in inducing guilty pleas' in J. Baldwin and A.K. Bottomley (eds) (1978) *q.v.*, pp. 116-28.

163

BANKOWSKI, Z. and MUNGHAM, G. (1976) *Images of Law* London, Routledge and Kegan Paul.

BANTON, M. (1964) *The Policeman in the Community* London, Tavistock.

BARNES, J.A. (1966) 'Durkheim's *Division of Labor in Society*' *Man* (new series) vol. 1, pp. 158-75.

BARNETT, R.E. (1977) 'Restitution: a new paradigm of criminal justice' *Ethics* vol. 87, pp. 279-301.

BATTLE, J.B. (1971) 'In search of the adversary system — the cooperative practices of private criminal defense attorneys' *Texas Law Review* vol. 50, pp. 60-118.

BECCARIA, C. (1764) *On Crimes and Punishment* trans. by H. Paolucci, Indianapolis, Bobbs-Merrill, 1963.

BECKER, H.S. (1963) *Outsiders: Studies in the Sociology of Deviance* New York, Free Press.

BELSON, W.A. (1975) *Juvenile Theft: the Causal Factors* London, Harper and Row.

BIANCHI, H. (1956) *Position and Subject-matter of Criminology: Inquiry Concerning Theoretical Criminology* Amsterdam, North-Holland.

BIDERMAN, A.D. and REISS, A.J. (1967) 'On exploring the "dark figure" of crime' *Annals of the American Academy of Political and Social Science* vol. 374, pp. 1-15.

BITTNER, E.A. (1967a) 'The police on skid-row: a study of peace keeping' *American Sociological Review* vol. 32, pp. 699-715.

BITTNER, E.A. (1967b) 'Police discretion in emergency apprehension of mentally ill persons' *Social Problems* vol. 14, pp. 278-92.

BITTNER, E.A. and PLATT, A.M. (1966) 'The meaning of punishment' *Issues in Criminology* vol. 2, pp. 79-99.

BLACK, D.J. (1970) 'Production of crime rates' *American Sociological Review* vol. 35, pp. 733-48.

BLACK, D.J. (1971) 'The social organization of arrest' *Stanford Law Review* vol. 23, pp. 1087-111.

BLACK, D.J. (1976) *The Behavior of Law* London, Academic Press.

BLUMBERG, A.S. (1967) *Criminal Justice* Chicago, Quadrangle Books.

BONGER, W.A. (1916) *Criminality and Economic Conditions* Boston, Little, Brown.

BORDUA, D.J. (ed) (1967) *The Police: Six Sociological Essays* New York, Wiley.

BOTTOMLEY, A.K. (1973) *Decisions in the Penal Process* London, Martin Robertson.

BOTTOMLEY, A.K. (1977) 'Conflict and communication in criminal justice' *Howard Journal of Penology and Crime Prevention* vol. 15 no. 3, pp.3-11.

BOTTOMLEY, A.K. (1978a) 'The failure of penal treatment — where do we go from here?' in J. Baldwin and A.K. Bottomley (eds) (1978) *q.v.*, pp. 238-46.

BOTTOMLEY, A.K. (1978b) 'The "justice model"; development and analysis' Paper presented to an interdisciplinary consultation in Manchester, April 1978.

BOTTOMLEY, A.K. and COLEMAN, C.A. (1976) 'Criminal statistics: the police role in the discovery and detection of crime' *International Journal of Criminology and Penology* vol. 4, pp. 33-58.

BOTTOMS, A.E. (1973) 'Methodological aspects of classification in criminology' in European Committee on Crime Problems *Collected Studies in Criminological Research* vol. X, Strasbourg, Council of Europe, pp. 27-76.

BOTTOMS, A.E. (1977) 'Reflections on the renaissance of dangerousness' *Howard Journal of Penology and Crime Prevention* vol. 16 pp. 70-96.

BOTTOMS, A.E. (1978) 'The coming crisis in British penology' Paper presented to an interdisciplinary consultation in Manchester, April 1978.

BOTTOMS, A.E. and McCLEAN, J.D. (1976) *Defendants in the Criminal Process* London, Routledge and Kegan Paul.

BOWLBY, J. (1965) *Child Care and the Growth of Love* Harmondsworth, Penguin Books.

BOX, S. (1971) *Deviance, Reality and Society* London, Holt, Rinehart and Winston.

BRODY, S.R. (1976) *The Effectiveness of Sentencing* London, HMSO.

BURT, C. (1944) *The Young Delinquent* (4th edn) London, University of London Press.

BUTLER COMMITTEE (1975) *Report of the Committee on Mentally Abnormal Offenders* Cmnd. 6244 London, HMSO.

CAIN, M. (1973) *Society and the Policeman's Role* London, Routledge and Kegan Paul.

CARLEN, P. (1976a) *Magistrates' Justice* London, Martin Robertson.

CARLEN, P. (1976b) *The Sociology of Law* Sociological Review Monograph No. 23, Keele, University of Keele.

CARSON, W.G. (1974) 'The sociology of crime and the emergence of criminal laws' in P. Rock and M. McIntosh (eds) (1974) *q.v.*, pp. 67-90.

CARSON, W.G. and WILES, P.N.P. (eds) (1971) *The Sociology of Crime and Delinquency in Britain: Vol. I The British Tradition* London, Martin Robertson.

CASPER, J.D. (1972) *American Criminal Justice: the Defendant's Perspective* Englewood Cliffs, Prentice-Hall.

CENTER, L.J. and SMITH, T.G. (1973) 'Crime statistics — can they be trusted?' *American Criminal Law Review* vol. 11, pp. 1045-86.

CHAMBLISS, W.J. (1964) 'A sociological analysis of the law of vagrancy' *Social Problems* vol. 12, pp. 67-77.

CHAMBLISS, W.J. (1975) 'Toward a political economy of crime' *Theory and Society* vol. 2, pp. 149-70.

CHAMBLISS, W.J. (1976) 'The state and criminal law' in W.J. Chambliss and M. Mankoff (eds) (1976) *q.v.*, pp. 66-106.

CHAMBLISS, W.J. and MANKOFF, M. (eds) (1976) *Whose Law? What Order? A Conflict Approach to Criminology* New York, Wiley.

CHAMBLISS, W.J. and SEIDMAN, R.B. (1971) *Law, Order and Power* Reading, Mass., Addison-Wesley.

CHATTERTON, M. (1976) 'Police in social control' in J.F.S. King (ed) *Control Without Custody?* Cambridge, Institute of Criminology, pp. 104-22.

CHEVALIER, L. (1973) *Labouring Classes and Dangerous Classes in Paris During the First Half of the Nineteenth Century* London, Routledge and Kegan Paul.

CHRISTIE, N. (1971) 'Scandinavian criminology facing the 1970s' in *Scandinavian Studies in Criminology* vol. 3 Universitetsforlaget, Oslo, pp. 121-49.

CHRISTIE, N. (1974) 'Utility and social values in court decisions on punishments' in R.G. Hood (ed) (1974d) *q.v.*, pp. 281-96.

CHRISTIE, N. (1977) 'Conflicts as property' *British Journal of Criminology* vol. 17, pp. 1-15.

CICOUREL, A.V. (1976) *The Social Organisation of Juvenile Justice* (rev. edn) London, Heinemann.

CLARKE, D.H. (1978) 'Marxism, justice and the justice model' *Contemporary Crises* vol. 2, pp. 27-62.

CLARKE, R.V.G. and SINCLAIR, I. (1974) 'Towards more effective treatment evaluation' in European Committee on Crime Problems *Collected Studies in Criminological Research* vol. XII Strasbourg, Council of Europe, pp. 53-87.

CLINARD, M.B. and QUINNEY, R. (1973) *Criminal Behavior Systems: A Typology* (rev. edn) New York, Holt, Rinehart and Winston.

CLOWARD, R.A. and OHLIN, L.E. (1960) *Delinquency and Opportunity: A Theory of Delinquent Gangs* New York, Free Press.

COHEN, A.K. (1951) 'Multiple factor approaches' in M.E. Wolfgang *et al.* (eds) *The Sociology of Crime and Delinquency* New York, Wiley, 1962, pp. 77-80.

COHEN, A.K. (1955) *Delinquent Boys: The Culture of the Gang* New York, Free Press.

COHEN, A.K. (1966) *Deviance and Control* Englewood Cliffs, Prentice-Hall.

COHEN, S. (1968) 'The politics of vandalism' *New Society* vol. 12, pp. 872-4.

COHEN, S. (1973a) 'Protest, unrest and delinquency: convergences in labels and behaviour' *International Journal of Criminology and Penology* vol. 1, pp. 117-28.

COHEN, S. (1973b) 'The failures of criminology' *The Listener* vol. 90 pp. 622-5.

COHEN, S. (1974) 'Criminology and the sociology of deviance in Britain' in P. Rock and M. McIntosh (eds) (1974) *q.v.*, pp. 1-40.

COLE, G.F. (1970) 'The decision to prosecute' *Law and Society Review* vol. 4, pp. 331-43.

COLE, G.F. (1973) *Politics and the Administration of Justice* Beverly Hills, Sage.

COLEMAN, C.A. and BOTTOMLEY, A.K. (1976) 'Police conceptions of crime and "no crime" ' *Criminal Law Review* June 1976, pp. 344-60.

CONNOR, W.D. (1972) *Deviance in Soviet Society: Crime, Delinquency and Alcoholism* New York, Columbia University Press.

CORNISH, D.B. (1971) *The Jury* Harmondsworth, Penguin Books.

CRESSEY, D.R. (1971) *Other People's Money: A Study in the Social*

Psychology of Embezzlement (rev. edn) Belmont, Calif., Wadsworth.
CUMMING, E., CUMMING, I.M. and EDELL, L. (1965) 'Policeman as philosopher, guide and friend' *Social Problems* vol. 12, pp. 276-86.

DAVIES, M. (1974) 'Social enquiry for the courts' *British Journal of Criminology* vol. 14, pp. 18-33.
DAVIS, K.C. (1969) *Discretionary justice: A Preliminary Inquiry* Baton Rouge, Louisiana State University Press.
DAVIS, K.C. (1975) *Police Discretion* St. Paul, Minn., West Publishing.
DAWSON, R.O. (1969) *Sentencing: the Decision as to Type, Length and Conditions of Sentence* Boston, Little, Brown.
DELL, S. (1971) *Silent in Court* London, Bell.
DESSAUR, C.I. (1971) *Foundations of Theory-formation in Criminology* The Hague, Mouton,
DRAPKIN, I. and VIANO, E. (eds) (1974a) *Victimology* Lexington,D. C. Heath.
DRAPKIN, I. and VIANO, E. (eds) (1974b) *Victimology: A New Focus* 5 vols., Lexington, D.C. Heath.
DRAY, W.H. (1957) *Laws and Explanation in History* London, Oxford University Press.
DURKHEIM, E. (1893) *The Division of Labour in Society* Trans. by G. Simpson, Glencoe, Free Press, 1933.
DURKHEIM, E. (1901) 'Two laws of penal evolution' trans. by T.A. Jones and A.T. Scull in *Economy and Society* vol. 2 1973, pp. 285-308.

EGLASH, A. (1958) 'Creative restitution: a broader meaning for an old term' *Journal of Criminal Law, Criminology and Police Science* vol. 48, pp. 619-22.
EHRLICH, I. (1972) 'The deterrent effect of criminal law enforcement' *Journal of Legal Studies* vol. 1, pp. 259-76.
ELLIS, H. (1901) *The Criminal* (3rd edn) London, Walter Scott.
EMERSON, R.M. (1969) *Judging Delinquents: Context and Process in Juvenile Court* Chicago, Aldine.
ERICSON, R.V. (1977) 'From social theory to penal practice: the liberal demise of criminological causes' *Canadian Journal of Criminology and Corrections* vol. 19, pp. 170-91.
ERIKSON, K.T. (1964) 'Notes on the sociology of deviance' in H.S. Becker (ed) *The Other Side* New York, Free Press, pp. 9-21.
ESER, A. (1966) 'The principle of "harm" in the concept of crime: a comparative analysis of the criminally protected legal interests' *Duquesne University Law Review* vol. 4, pp. 345-417.
EWING, A.C. (1929) *The Morality of Punishment* London, Kegan Paul.
EYSENCK, H. (1977) *Crime and Personality* (3rd edn.) London, Routledge and Kegan Paul.

FEINBERG, J. (1970) *Doing and Deserving: Essays in the Theory of Responsibility* Princeton, Princeton University Press.

FERDINAND, T.N. (1966) *Typologies of Delinquency: A Critical Analysis* New York, Random House.

FERRI, E. (1913) *The Positive School of Criminology* Chicago, C.H. Kerr.

FERRI, E. (1917) *Criminal Sociology* Boston, Little, Brown.

FIELD, E. (1967) *A Validation Study of Hewitt and Jenkins' Hypothesis* London, HMSO.

FOGEL, D. (1975) *"We are the Living Proof . . .": the Justice Model for Corrections* Cincinnati, Anderson.

FORD, J. (1975) *Paradigms and Fairy Tales: An Introduction to the Science of Meanings* 2 vols., London, Routledge and Kegan Paul.

FOUCAULT, M. (1977) *Discipline and Punish: the Birth of the Prison* London, Allen Lane.

FRANKEL, M.E. (1973) *Criminal Sentences: Law without Order* New York, Hill and Wang.

FRIEDLANDER, K. (1947) *The Psychoanalytical Approach to Juvenile Delinquency* London, Routledge and Kegan Paul.

GAROFALO, R. (1914) *Criminology* Boston, Little, Brown.

GIBBENS, T.C.N. (1963) *Psychiatric Studies of Borstal Lads* London, Oxford University Press.

GIBBONS, D.C. (1965) *Changing the Lawbreaker* Englewood Cliffs, Prentice-Hall.

GIBBONS, D.C. (1971) 'Observations on the study of crime causation' *American Journal of Sociology* vol. 77, pp. 262-78.

GIBBONS, D.C. (1975) 'Offender typologies — two decades later' *British Journal of Criminology* vol. 15, pp. 140-56.

GIBBS, J.P. (1975) *Crime, Punishment and Deterrence* Amsterdam, Elsevier.

GINSBERG, M. (1965) *On Justice in Society* Harmondsworth, Penguin Books.

GLASER, B.G. and STRAUSS, A.L. (1967) *The Discovery of Grounded Theory: Strategies for Qualitative Research* Chicago, Aldine.

GLUECK, S. (1956) 'Theory and fact in criminology' *British Journal of Delinquency* vol. 7, pp. 92-109.

GLUECK, S. and GLUECK, E. (1950) *Unraveling Juvenile Delinquency* Cambridge, Mass., Harvard University Press.

GLUECK, S. and GLUECK, E. (1965) 'Varieties of delinquent types' *British Journal of Criminology* vol. 5, pp. 236-48, 388-405.

GOLD, M. (1970) *Delinquent Behavior in an American City* Belmont, Calif., Brooks/Cole.

GOLDSTEIN, H. (1977) *Policing a Free Society* Cambridge, Mass., Ballinger.

GOLDSTEIN, J. (1960) 'Police discretion not to invoke the criminal process: low-visibility decisions in the administration of justice' *Yale Law Journal* vol. 69, pp. 543-94.

GORING, C.B. (1913) *The English Convict: A Statistical Study* London, HMSO.

GOULD, L.C. (1968) 'Who defines delinquency: a comparison of self-reported and officially-reported indices of delinquency for three racial groups' *Social Problems* vol. 16, pp. 325-36.

GREENBERG, D.F. (1975) 'The incapacitative effect of imprisonment: some estimates' *Law and Society Review* vol. 9, pp. 541-80.

GRIFFITH, J.A.G. (1977) *The Politics of the Judiciary* London, Fontana.

GRIFFITHS, J. (1970) 'Ideology in criminal procedure, *or* A third "model" of the criminal process' *Yale Law Journal* vol. 79, pp. 359-417.

HALL, J. (1952) *Theft, Law and Society* (2nd edn) Indianapolis, Bobbs-Merrill.

HALL, J. (1960) *General Principles of Criminal Law* (2nd edn) Indianapolis, Bobbs-Merrill.

HARDIKER, P. (1977) 'Social work ideologies in the probation service' *British Journal of Social Work* vol. 7, pp. 131-54.

HART, H.L.A. (1968) *Punishment and Responsibility: Essays in the Philosophy of Law* London, Oxford University Press.

HART, H.L.A. and HONORE, A.M. (1959) *Causation in the Law.* London, Oxford University Press.

HART, H.M. (1958) 'The aims of the criminal law' *Law and Contemporary Problems* vol. 23, pp. 401–41.

HARTJEN, C.A. (1972) 'Legalism and humanism: a reply to the Schwendingers' *Issues in Criminology* vol. 7, pp. 59-69

HAY, D. *et al.* (1975) *Albion's Fatal Tree: Crime and Society in Eighteenth-Century England* London, Allen Lane.

HEMPEL, C.G. (1965) *Aspects of Scientific Explanation* New York, Free Press.

HEMPEL, C.G. (1966) 'Explanation in science and in history' in W.H. Dray (ed) *Philosophical Analysis and History* New York, Harper and Row, pp. 95-126.

HEWITT, L.E. and JENKINS, R.L. (1946) *Fundamental Patterns of Maladjustment: The Dynamics of their Origin* Illinois, D.H. Green.

HINDELANG, M. (1976) *Criminal Victimization in Eight American Cities* Cambridge, Mass., Ballinger.

HIRSCHI, T. and SELVIN, H.C. (1973) *Principles of Survey Analysis* New York, Free Press.

HOLDAWAY, S. (1977) 'Changes in urban policing' *British Journal of Sociology* vol. 28, pp. 119-37.

HOME OFFICE (1961) *Report of the Interdepartmental Committee on the Business of the Criminal Courts* Cmnd. 1289 London, HMSO.

HOME OFFICE (1977) *Prisons and the Prisoner* London, HMSO.

HOOD, R.G. (1962) *Sentencing in Magistrates' Courts* London, Stevens.

HOOD, R.G. (1972) *Sentencing the Motoring Offender* London, Heinemann.

HOOD, R.G. (1974a) 'Some fundamental dilemmas of the English parole system and a suggestion for an alternative structure' in D.A. Thomas (ed) *Parole: Its Implications for the Criminal Justice and Penal Systems* Cambridge, Institute of Criminology, pp. 1-17.

HOOD, R.G. (1974b) *Tolerance and the Tariff: Some Reflections on the Time Prisoners Serve in Custody* London, NACRO.

HOOD, R.G. (1974c) 'Young Adult Offenders: comments on the Report of the Advisory Council on the Penal System' *British Journal of Criminology* vol. 14, pp. 388-95.

HOOD, R.G. (ed) (1974d)   *Crime, Criminology and Public Policy* London, Heinemann.

HOOD, R.G. and SPARKS, R.F. (1970)   *Key Issues in Criminology* London, Weidenfeld and Nicolson.

HOROWITZ, I.L. and LIEBOWITZ, M. (1968)   'Social deviance and political marginality: toward a redefinition of the relation between sociology and politics' *Social Problems* vol. 15, pp. 280-96.

HOWARD LEAGUE FOR PENAL REFORM (1977)   *Making Amends: Criminals, Victims and Society* Chichester, Barry Rose.

JEFFERY, C.R. (1956a)   'The structure of American criminological thinking' *Journal of Criminal Law. Criminology and Police Science* vol. 46, pp. 658-72.

JEFFERY, C.R. (1956b)   'Crime, law and social structure' *Journal of Criminal Law, Criminology and Police Science* vol. 47, pp. 423-35.

JEFFERY, C.R. (1957)   'The development of crime in early English society' *Journal of Criminal Law, Criminology and Police Science* vol. 47, pp. 647-66.

JEFFERY, C.R. (1959a)   'An integrated theory of crime and criminal behavior' *Journal of Criminal Law, Criminology and Police Science.* vol. 49, pp. 533-52.

JEFFERY, C.R. (1959b)   'Historical development of criminology' *Journal of Criminal Law, Criminology and Police Science* vol. 50, pp. 3-19, reprinted in H. Mannheim (ed) (1960) *q.v.*, pp. 364-94.

JEFFERY, C.R. (1971)   *Crime Prevention Through Environmental Design* Beverly Hills, Sage.

JEUDWINE, J.W. (1917)   *Tort, Crime, and Police in Mediaeval Britain* London, Williams and Norgate.

JONES, H. (1958)   'Approaches to an ecological study' *British Journal of Delinquency* vol. 8, pp. 277-93.

KALVEN, H. and ZEISEL, H. (1966)   *The American Jury* Chicago, University of Chicago Press.

KENNEDY, M.C. (1970)   'Beyond incrimination: some neglected facets of the theory of punishment' *Catalyst* no. 5, pp. 1-37, reprinted in W.J. Chambliss and M. Mankoff (eds) (1976) *q.v.*, pp. 34-64.

KITSUSE, J.I. (1964)   'Social reaction to deviant behavior: problems of theory and method' in H.S. Becker (ed) *The Other Side* New York, Free Press, pp. 87-102.

KITSUSE, J.I. and CICOUREL, A.V. (1963)   'A note on the use of official statistics' *Social Problems* vol. 11, pp. 131-9.

KITTRIE, N.N. (1971)   *The Right to be Different: Deviance and Enforced Therapy* Baltimore, John Hopkins.

KLEINIG, J. (1973)   *Punishment and Desert* The Hague, Martinus Nijhoff.

KOZOL, H.L., BOUCHER, R.J. and GAROFALO, R.F. (1972)   'The diagnosis and treatment of dangerousness' *Crime and Delinquency* vol. 18, p. 371-92.

KWARTLER, R. (1977)   *Behind Bars: Prisons in America* New York, Vintage Books.

LAFAVE, W.R. (1965)   *Arrest: the Decision to Take a Suspect into Custody* Boston, Little, Brown.

LESSNOFF, M. (1974)   *The Structure of Social Science: A Philosophical Introduction* London, Allen and Unwin.

LEWIS, C.S. (1953)   'The humanitarian theory of punishment' *Res Judicatae* vol. 6, pp. 224-30.

LINDESMITH, A.R. and LEVIN, Y. (1937a)   'English ecology and criminology of the past century' *Journal of Criminal Law, Criminology and Police Science* vol. 27, pp. 801-16.

LINDESMITH, A.R. and LEVIN, Y. (1937b)   'The Lombrosian myth in criminology' *American Journal of Sociology* vol. 42, pp. 653-71.

LIPTON, D., MARTINSON, R. and WILKS, J. (1975)   *Effectiveness of Correctional Treatment: A Survey of Evaluation Studies* New York, Praeger.

LOGAN, C.H. (1972)   'Evaluation research in crime and delinquency' *Journal of Criminal Law, Criminology and Police Science* vol. 63, pp.378-87.

LOMBROSO, C. (1918)   *Crime: Its Causes and Remedies* Boston, Little, Brown.

LOW, C. (1978)   'The sociology of criminal justice: progress and prospects' in J. Baldwin and A.K. Bottomley (eds) (1978) *q.v.*, pp. 7-22.

MCBARNET, D.J. (1976)   'Pre-trial procedures and the construction of conviction' in P. Carlen (ed) (1976) *q.v.*, pp. 172-201.

MCBARNET, D.J. (1977)   'The police and the state: arrest, legality and the law' Paper presented at the British Sociological Association Conference, April 1977.

MCBARNET, D.J. (1978)   'False dichotomies in criminal justice research' in J. Baldwin and A.K. Bottomley (eds) (1978) *q.v.*, pp. 23-34.

MCCABE, S. and PURVES, R. (1972a)   *By-passing the Jury* Oxford, Blackwell.

MCCABE, S. and PURVES, R. (1972b) *The Jury at Work* Oxford, Blackwell.

MCCABE, S. and PURVES, R. (1974)   *The Shadow Jury at Work* Oxford, Blackwell.

MCDONALD, L. (1976)   *The Sociology of Law and Order* London, Faber and Faber.

MCDONALD, W.F. (ed) (1976)   *Criminal Justice and the Victim* Beverly Hills, Sage.

MAKELA, K. (1975)   'The societal tasks of the system of penal law' in H. Bianchi *et al.* (eds) *Deviance and Control in Europe* New York, Wiley, pp. 157-74.

MANNHEIM, H. (1960)   *Pioneers in Criminology* London, Stevens.

MANNHEIM, H. (1965)   *Comparative Criminology* 2 vols., London, Routledge and Kegan Paul.

MANNHEIM, H. and WILKINS, L.T. (1955)   *Prediction Methods in Relation to Borstal Training* London, HMSO.

MARTINSON, R. (1974)   'What works? — questions and answers about prison reform' *The Public Interest* Spring 1974, pp. 22-54.

MATZA, D.M. (1964)   *Delinquency and Drift* New York, Wiley.

MATZA, D.M. (1969)   *Becoming Deviant* Englewood Cliffs, Prentice-Hall.

MAYHEW, P. *et al.* (1976)   *Crime as Opportunity* London, HMSO.

MAYS, J.B. (1954)   *Growing Up in the City* Liverpool, University of Liverpool Press.

MERTON, R.K. (1938)   'Social structure and anomie' *American Sociological Review* vol. 3, pp. 672-82.

MICHAEL, J. and ADLER, M. (1933)   *Crime, Law and Social Science* London, Kegan Paul.

MILLER, F.W. (1969)   *Prosecution: The Decision to Charge a Suspect with a Crime* Boston, Little, Brown.

MILLER, W.B. (1958)   'Lower class culture as a generating milieu of gang delinquency' *Journal of Social Issues* vol. 14, pp. 5-19.

MILLER, W.B. (1973)   'Ideology and criminal justice policy: some current issues' *Journal of Criminal Law and Criminology* vol. 64, pp. 141-62.

MOBERLY, W. (1968)   *The Ethics of Punishment* London, Faber and Faber.

MORRIS, N. (1974)   *The Future of Imprisonment* Chicago, University of Chicago Press.

MORRIS, N. and HAWKINS, G. (1970)   *The Honest Politician's Guide to Crime Control* Chicago, University of Chicago Press.

MORRIS, T. (1957)   *The Criminal Area* London, Routledge and Kegan Paul.

MORRIS, T. (1976)   *Deviance and Control: The Secular Heresy* London, Hutchinson.

MUELLER, G.O.W. (1955)   'Tort, crime and the primitive' *Journal of Criminal Law, Criminology and Police Science* vol. 46, pp. 303-32.

NELSON, W.E. (1967)   'Emerging notions of modern criminal law in the revolutionary era: an historical perspective' *New York University Law Review* vol. 42, pp. 450-82.

NEUBAUER, D.W. (1974)   *Criminal Justice in Middle America* Morristown, N.J., General Learning Press.

NEWMAN, D.J. (1958)   'White-collar crime' *Law and Contemporary Problems* vol. 23, pp. 735-53.

NEWMAN, D.J. (1966)   *Conviction: the Determination of Guilt or Innocence Without Trial* Boston, Little, Brown.

NEWMAN, D.J. (1975)   *Introduction to Criminal Justice* Philadelphia, Lippincott.

NEWMAN, O. (1972)   *Defensible Space: People and Design in the Violent City* London, Architectural Press.

NIEDERHOFFER, A. (1969)   *Behind the Shield: The Police in Urban Society* New York, Anchor Books.

PACKER, H.L. (1969) *The Limits of the Criminal Sanction* Stanford, Stanford University Press.

PALMER, T. (1975) 'Martinson revisited' *Journal of Research in Crime and Delinquency* vol. 12, pp. 133-52.

PATERSON, A.A. (1974) 'Judges: a political elite?' *British Journal of Law and Society* vol. 1, pp. 118-35.

PEPINSKY, H.E. (1976) *Crime and Conflict: A Study of Law and Society* London, Martin Robertson.

PILIAVIN, I. and BRIAR, S. (1964) 'Police encounters with juveniles' *American Journal of Sociology* vol. 70, pp. 206-14.

PLATT, A.M. (1975) 'Prospects for a radical criminology in the USA' in I. Taylor, P. Walton and J. Young (eds) (1975) *q.v.*, pp. 95-112.

PHILLIPSON, M. (1971) *Sociological Aspects of Crime and Delinquency* London, Routledge and Kegan Paul.

QUINNEY, R. (1964a) 'Crime in political perspective' *American Behavioral Scientist* vol. 8, pp. 19-22.

QUINNEY, R. (1964b) 'The study of white-collar crime: toward a reorientation in theory and research' *Journal of Criminal Law, Criminology and Police Science* vol. 55, pp. 208-14.

QUINNEY, R. (1970) *The Social Reality of Crime* Boston, Little, Brown.

QUINNEY, R. (1974) *Critique of Legal Order: Crime Control in Capitalist Society* Boston, Little, Brown.

QUINNEY, R. and WILDEMAN, J. (1977) *The Problem of Crime: A Critical Introduction to Criminology* (2nd edn) New York, Harper and Row.

RADZINOWICZ, L. (1966) *Ideology and Crime: A Study of Crime in its Social and Historical Context* London, Heinemann.

RAWLS, J. (1972) *A Theory of Justice* London, Oxford University Press.

RAWSON, R.W. (1839) 'An inquiry into the statistics of crime in England and Wales' *Journal of the Statistical Society of London* vol. 2, pp. 316-44.

REISS, A.J. (1971) *The Police and the Public* New Haven, Yale University Press.

REISS, A.J. (1974) 'Citizen access to criminal justice' *British Journal of Law and Society* vol. 1, pp. 50-74.

REISS, A.J. and BLACK, D.J. (1967) 'Interrogation and the criminal process' *Annals of the American Academy of Political and Social Science* vol. 374, pp. 47-57.

REISS, A.J. and BORDUA, D.J. (1967) 'Environment and the police: a perspective on the police' in D.J. Bordua (ed) (1967) *q.v.*, pp. 25-55.

REASONS, C.E. (1973) 'The politicizing of crime, the criminal and the criminologist' *Journal of Criminal Law and Criminology* vol. 64, pp. 471-7.

ROBINSON, W.S. (1951) 'The logical structure of analytical induction' *American Sociological Review* vol. 16, pp. 812-18.

ROCK, P. (1973) *Deviant Behaviour* London, Hutchinson.

ROCK, P. and MCINTOSH, M. (eds) (1974) *Deviance and Social Control* London, Tavistock.

ROEBUCK, J.B. (1967) *Criminal Typology* Springfield, Thomas.
ROSS, A. (1975) *On Guilt, Responsibility and Punishment* London, Stevens.
ROSS, H.L. (1960) 'Traffic law violation: a folk crime' *Social Problems* vol. 8, pp. 231-41.
RUBINSTEIN, J. (1973) *City Police* New York, Ballantine Books.
RUSCHE, G. and KIRCHHEIMER, O. (1939) *Punishment and Social Structure* New York, Columbia University Press.
RUTTER, M. (1972) *Maternal Deprivation Reassessed* Harmondsworth, Penguin Books.
RYAN, A. (1970) *The Philosophy of the Social Sciences* London, Macmillan.

SCHAFER, S. (1960) *Restitution to Victims of Crime* London, Stevens.
SCHAFER, S. (1968) *The Victim and his Criminal: A Study in Functional Responsibility* New York, Random House.
SCHAFER, S. (1969) *Theories in Criminology* New York, Random House.
SCHAFER, S. (1971) 'The concept of the political criminal' *Journal of Criminal Law, Criminology and Police Science* vol. 62, pp. 380-87.
SCHAFER, S. (1974) *The Political Criminal* Glencoe, Free Press.
SCHUR, E.M. (1973) *Radical Non-intervention: Rethinking the Delinquency Problem* Englewood Cliffs, Prentice-Hall.
SCHWARTZ, R.D. and MILLER, J.C. (1964) 'Legal evolution and societal complexity' *American Journal of Sociology* vol. 70, pp. 159-69.
SCHWENDINGER, H. and SCHWENDINGER, J. (1970) 'Defenders of order or guardians of human rights?' *Issues in Criminology* vol. 5, pp. 123-57.
SCOTTISH COUNCIL ON CRIME (1975) *Crime and the Prevention of Crime* London, HMSO.
SEIDMAN, D. and COUZENS, M. (1974) 'Getting the crime rate down: political pressure and crime reporting' *Law and Society Review* vol. 8, pp. 457-93.
SELLIN, T. (1931) 'The basis of a crime index' *Journal of Criminal Law, Criminology and Police Science* vol. 22, pp. 335-56.
SELLIN, T. (1938) *Culture Conflict and Crime* New York, Social Science Research Council.
SELLIN, T. (1951) 'The significance of records of crime' *The Law Quarterly Review* vol. 67, pp. 489-504.
SELLIN, T. and WOLFGANG, M.E. (1964) *The Measurement of Delinquency* New York, Wiley.
SETHI, D. (1976) Book review of W.A. Belson *Juvenile Theft: the Causal Factors, British Journal of Criminology* vol. 16, pp. 405-7.
SHAW, C. (1929) *Delinquency Areas* Chicago, University of Chicago Press.
SHAW, C. and MCKAY, H. (1969) *Juvenile Delinquency in Urban Areas* (rev. edn) Chicago, University of Chicago Press.
SHELEFF, L.S. (1975) 'From restitutive law to repressive law: Durkheim's *The Division of Labour in Society* revisited' *Archives Européenne de Sociologie* vol. 16, pp. 16-45.
SIMON, F.H. (1971) *Prediction Methods in Criminology* London, HMSO.

SKOGAN, W.G. (ed) (1976) *Sample Surveys of the Victims of Crime* Cambridge, Mass., Ballinger.

SKOLNICK, J.H. (1966) *Justice Without Trial: Law Enforcement in Democratic Society* New York, Wiley.

SKOLNICK, J.H. (1967) 'Social control in the adversary system' *Journal of Conflict Resolution* vol. 11, pp. 52-70.

SKOLNICK, J.H. (1969) *The Politics of Protest* New York, Simon and Schuster.

SPARKS, R.F., GENN, H. and DODD, D. (1977) *Surveying Victims* London, Wiley.

SPITZER, S. (1975) 'Punishment and social organization: a study of Durkheim's theory of penal evolution, *Law and Society Review* vol. 9, pp. 613-37.

STEADMAN, H.J. and COCOZZA, J.J. (1974) *Careers of the Criminally Insane: Excessive Control of Deviance* Lexington, D.C. Heath.

SUDNOW, D. (1965) 'Normal crimes: sociological features of the penal code in a public defender office' *Social Problems* vol. 12, pp. 255-76.

SULLIVAN, D.C. and SIEGEL, L.J. (1972) 'How police use information to make decisions — an application of decision games' *Crime and Delinquency* vol. 18, pp. 253-62.

SUTHERLAND, E.H. (1937) *The Professional Thief* Chicago, University of Chicago Press.

SUTHERLAND, E.H. (1940) 'White-collar criminality' *American Sociological Review* vol. 5, pp. 1-12.

SUTHERLAND, E.H. (1945) 'Is "white-collar crime" crime?' *American Sociological Review* vol. 10, pp. 132-9.

SUTHERLAND, E.H. (1934, 1939, 1947) *Principles of Criminology* New York, Lippincott.

SUTHERLAND, E.H. (1949) *White-collar Crime* New York, Dryden Press.

SUTHERLAND, E.H. and CRESSEY, D.R. (1970) *Principles of Criminology* New York, Lippincott.

TAPPAN, P.W. (1947) 'Who is the criminal?' *American Sociological Review* vol. 12 pp. 96-102.

TARDE, G. (1912) *Penal Philosophy* Boston, Little, Brown.

TAYLOR, I., WALTON, P. and YOUNG, J. (1973) *The New Criminology* London, Routledge and Kegan Paul.

TAYLOR, I., WALTON, P. and YOUNG, J. (eds) (1975) *Critical Criminology* London, Routledge and Kegan Paul.

THOMPSON, E.P. (1975) *Whigs and Hunters: the Origins of the Black Act* London, Allen Lane.

TIFFANY, L.P. *et al.* (1967) *Detection of Crime: Stopping and Questioning, Search and Seizure, Encouragement and Entrapment* Boston, Little, Brown.

TITTLE, C.R. and LOGAN, C.H. (1973) 'Sanctions and deviance: evidence and remaining questions' *Law and Society Review* vol. 7, pp. 371-92.

TURNER, R.H. (1953) 'The quest for universals in sociological research' *American Sociological Review* vol. 18, pp. 604-11.

VAN BEMMELEN, J.M. (1952) 'The constancy of crime' *British Journal of Delinquency* vol. 2, pp. 208-28.

VOLD, G.B. (1958) *Theoretical Criminology* London, Oxford University Press.

VON HIRSCH, A. (1976) *Doing Justice: the Choice of Punishments* Report confinement of convicted persons' *Buffalo Law Review* vol. 21, pp. 717-58.

VON HIRSCH, A. (1976) *Doing Justice: the Choice of Punishments* report of the Committee for the Study of Incarceration, New York, Hill and Wang.

WALKER, N.D. (1966) 'A century of causal theory' in H. Klare and D. Haxby (eds) *Frontiers of Criminology* London, Pergamon, pp. 3-18.

WALKER, N.D. (1974) 'Lost causes in criminology' in R.G. Hood (ed) (1974d) *q.v.*, pp. 47-62.

WALKER, N.D. (ed) (1975) *The British Jury System* Cambridge, Institute of Criminology.

WALKER, N.D. (1977) *Behaviour and Misbehaviour: Explanations and non-explanations* Oxford, Blackwell.

WALSH, J.L. (1977) 'Career styles and police behavior' in D.H. Bayley (ed) *Police and Society*, Beverly Hills, Sage, pp. 149-75.

WARD, C. (ed) (1973) *Vandalism* London, Architectural Press.

WEBER, M. (1949) *The Methodology of the Social Sciences* New York, Free Press.

WEBER, M. (1964) *The Theory of Social and Economic Organization* New York, Free Press.

WENK, E., ROBISON, J. and SMITH, G.W. (1972) 'Can violence be predicted?' *Crime and Delinquency* vol. 18, pp. 393-402.

WEST, D.J. and FARRINGTON, D.P. (1969) *Present Conduct and Future Delinquency* London, Heinemann.

WEST, D.J. and FARRINGTON, D.P. (1973) *Who Becomes Delinquent?* London, Heinemann.

WEST, D.J. and FARRINGTON, D.P. (1977) *The Delinquent Way of Life* London, Heinemann.

WESTLEY, W.A. (1953) 'Violence and the police' *American Journal of Sociology* vol. 59, pp. 34-41.

WESTLEY, W.A. (1970) *Violence and the Police: A Sociological Study of Law, Custom and Morality* Cambridge, Mass., MIT Press.

WHEELER, S. (1962) 'The social sources of criminology' *Sociological Inquiry* vol. 32, pp. 139-59.

WHEELER, S. (1967) 'Criminal statistics: a reformulation of the problem' *Journal of Criminal Law, Criminology and Police Science* vol. 58, pp. 317-24.

WILES, P.N.P. (ed) (1976) *The Sociology of Crime and Delinquency in Britain Vol. II: The New Criminologies* London, Martin Robertson.

WILES, P.N.P. and BEYLEVELD, D. (1975) 'Man and method in David Matza's *Becoming Deviant*' *British Journal of Criminology* vol. 15, pp. 111-27.

WILKINS, L.T. (1964)   *Social Deviance: Social Policy, Action and Research* London, Tavistock.

WILKINS, L.T. (1965)   'New thinking in criminal statistics' *Journal of Criminal Law, Criminology and Police Science* vol. 56, pp. 277-84.

WILKINS, L.T. (1968)   'The concept of cause in criminology' *Issues in Criminology* vol. 3, pp. 147-65.

WILKINS, L.T. (1973)   'Crime and criminal justice at the turn of the century' in *Annals of the American Academy of Political and Social Science* vol. 408, pp. 13-26.

WILKINS, L.T. (1974)   'Directions for corrections' *Proceedings of the American Philosophical Society* vol. 118, pp. 235-47, reprinted in R.M. Carter and L.T. Wilkins (eds) *Probation, Parole and Community Corrections* (2nd edn) New York, Wiley, 1976, pp. 56-76.

WILKINS, L.T. and CHANDLER, A. (1965)   'Confidence and competence in decision-making' *British Journal of Criminology* vol. 5, pp. 22-35.

WILLIAMS, J.R. and GOLD, M. (1972)   'From delinquent behavior to official delinquency' *Social Problems* vol. 20, pp. 209-29.

WOLFGANG, M.E. (1963)   'Criminology and the criminologist' *Journal of Criminal Law, Criminology and Police Science* vol. 54, pp. 155-62.

WILSON, J.Q. (1963)   'The police and their problems' in *Public Policy: Vol. XII* Cambridge, Mass., Harvard University Press, reprinted in J.R. Klonoski and R.I. Mendelsohn (eds) *The Politics of Local Justice* Boston, Little, Brown 1970, pp. 161-74.

WILSON, J.Q. (1968)   *Varieties of Police Behavior* Cambridge, Mass., Harvard University Press.

WILSON, J.Q. (1975)   *Thinking About Crime* New York, Basic Books.

WILSON, R.J. (1973)   'British judges as political actors' *International Journal of Criminology and Penology* vol. 1, pp. 197-215.

WOOTTON, B. (1959)   *Social Science and Social Pathology* London, Allen and Unwin.

WORKING PARTY ON THE DANGEROUS OFFENDER (1977)   *The Dangerous Offender: A Consultative Document* Cambridge, Institute of Criminology.

WRIGHT, M. (1977)   'Nobody came: criminal justice and the needs of victims' *Howard Journal of Penology and Crime Prevention* vol. 16, pp. 22-31.

ZIMRING, F.E. and HAWKINS, G.J. (1973)   *Deterrence: the Legal Threat in Crime Control* Chicago, University of Chicago Press.

ZNANIECKI, F. (1928)   'Social research in criminology' *Sociology and Social Research* vol. 12, pp. 307-22.

ZNANIECKI, F. (1934)   *The Method of Sociology* New York, Farrar and Rinehart.

ZNANIECKI, F. (1969)   *On Humanistic Sociology: Selected Papers* edited by R. Bierstedt, Chicago, University of Chicago Press.

178

Index of Names

Index of Subjects